How to Get Started
When You Don't Know
Where to Begin

Patricia Hoyt | # How to Get Started When You Don't Know Where to Begin

Harcourt Brace Jovanovich, New York and London

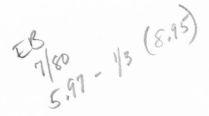

Requests for permission to make copies of any part
of the work should be mailed to:
Permissions, Harcourt Brace Jovanovich, Inc.,
757 Third Avenue, New York, N.Y. 10017

Illustrations have been provided through the courtesy of the following:
Internal Revenue Service, pages 43, 45, 47, and 48
United Bank of Arizona, page 67
New York City Department of Health, page 129
Safety Administration of the United States Department of the Interior,
pages 130, 131, 132, 133 (adapted), and 135
General Services Administration, page 184

Printed in the United States of America

Library of Congress Catalog Card Number: 79–3762
ISBN: 0-15-232263-9

First edition

B C D E

This book is dedicated to the men

in my life—my husband, Al, and

our four sons, Mike, Ed, Jim, and John

Contents

Foreword

There's one thing you've got to understand. I never intended to write this book. I never intended to write anything at all. The truth is, this book is the product of a conspiracy. I have four sons. They used to range from small to middle sized. Later they ranged from oversized to huge. Now they range from Phoenix to all points around the country.

I kept getting phone calls (collect, naturally). "Hey, Mom," one of them would say. "How do I establish credit? This guy won't sell me a TV set."

"Gee, I got a swell apartment, Mom. What should I buy before I move in? I've only got thirty-five dollars left. . . . "

"What do you mean I've got to get insurance? That old heap isn't worth a hundred bucks!"

Get the idea?

In self-defense, and because I couldn't afford the telephone bills, I did the research and wrote them the answers. The research led me through thousands of fragmentary sources, ranging from United States government publications to trade journals, company literature, Red Cross pamphlets, and a lot more. I was continually surprised at the vast amount to be learned about each subject, and I began to realize that knowledge of any subject is beyond the scope of a single book. So I picked and chose, going into greater or lesser detail as the subject warranted. The result, I believe, is a book that will be helpful.

In several instances I have given step-by-step procedures and have shown application forms, checks, and illustrations of other forms that you may come across in your day-to-day activities. I'd like to point out, however, that different companies, banks, and areas of the country follow slightly different procedures and use slightly different forms. Those discussed and shown in this book are meant to serve only as guidelines. They should be helpful, nevertheless, since the basic concepts explained can be applied to all of them.

Acknowledgments

I gratefully acknowledge the help and support of Dorothy Carter, Ed Hoyt, Allan G. Gilloon, M.D., Irene Feill, Genevieve Hoyt, Dorothy Trower and most of all, my husband, Al, who provided the encouragement and the environment that made this book possible.

I also wish to extend thanks to the many organizations that provided information and assistance, including, the National Safety Council, various Federal Information Centers, the California Department of Consumer Affairs, the National Red Cross, the Internal Revenue Service, the Federal Trade Commission, the United States Civil Service Commission, the United States Department of Economic Security, the United States General Services Administration, the United States Consumer Information Center, and the United Bank of Arizona.

How to Get Started When You Don't Know Where to Begin

1 | Training for the Job

Free at last! Wherever you're coming from—just graduated, just moved into a new area, just come of age, just got kicked out into the cold—welcome! Welcome to the whole new life that starts today, to the world of making your own way.

Getting started often means getting a job, a source of income. But before you rush out, pause a moment. You may have forty or fifty years of working ahead of you. Think about the kind of work you would enjoy. Set a goal. A goal is nothing more than a dream with a timetable. Stretch your imagination. Take time to get to know yourself. Make a list of your needs, abilities, and interests. Include the hobbies, jobs, and activities that have given you the most satisfaction. Let this list help you determine what makes you happy and what you do best. You'll identify milestones on the way to your goal. These are preliminary goals. They could be training you'll need, additional schooling, a series of carefully planned jobs, or any of a dozen intermediate objectives leading to your major goal. Write these down, too. They'll be an invaluable road map, both now and in the future. Be prepared to modify or change your ambitions as time goes on. Most of us do. The important thing is to *have* a purpose so that you don't drift aimlessly.

Once your goals are set, you'll begin thinking about training for the right job. In today's complex world, job opportunities are almost endless. How to go about qualifying for them can be bewildering. You have a number of basic options and, within each of these, a number of approaches. The options are: continuing your education, getting vocational training, getting a job, or a combination of these.

We'll discuss getting a job in the next chapter. Here we'll look at the first two options. And since there's no point in training for a job that won't be available by the time you qualify for it, we'll discuss how to find out what jobs *will* be available.

JOB OUTLOOK

Once upon a time a promising young lad apprenticed himself to a master craftsman whose specialty was making buggy whips, but Henry Ford's first production line put an end to that career. Then the young man found a job in a factory that made cranks to start Ford cars. But Charles Kettering's electric starter made that job obsolete, and he decided to go into the radio business. He trained to blow glass to make radio vacuum tubes. The development of the transistor ended that career. Next, he went back to school to brush up his early skill in mathematics in order to get a night job adding up accounts at a bank. Then a computer took that job away.

You can avoid such problems through a little advance planning. The following publications and organizations can give you an overview of current and future career opportunities.

United States Government Publications

The job market is constantly changing, so the United States Department of Labor publishes a book every two years called *Occupational Outlook Handbook,* which can be found in your local library. This handbook lists almost every job available, the working conditions, and future employment possibilities. It would be fun just to look through it and see all the opportunities that are open to you.

The Labor Department also publishes five free pamphlets, which list the occupations available, qualifications and training necessary for each, and employment opportunities and trends through 1985. The jobs are classified as follows:

- Jobs for which a high school education is preferred but not essential
- Jobs for which a high school education is generally required
- Jobs for which apprenticeships are available

- Jobs for which junior college, technical institute, or other specialized training is usually required
- Jobs for which a college education is usually required

Call the Federal Information Center (see Chapter 12) and ask where you can get these pamphlets in your state, or write to:
United States Department of Labor
Washington, D.C. 20212

State Publications

Some states have job-seeker publications of their own, listing:

- Number of jobs available in your field
- Job descriptions
- Training
- Salary
- Lines of advancement
- Locations of jobs
- Employment outlook

Your state Department of Labor or state employment agency should be able to help you find these guides.

Trade Organization and Society Publications

Organizations and societies often publish free pamphlets about the occupations they represent. Your librarian will help you identify the appropriate organization and find its address. If, for example, you are interested in becoming a dietician, you can write to the American Dietetic Association, asking for information on jobs, training, and scholarships available.

There is a reference book in your local library called *Encyclopedia of Associations* in which you can look up the address.

CONTINUING YOUR EDUCATION

If the job you want requires training, various programs are available. Your library, former school, family, and friends can help you pick the right one for *you.*

I'll name some of the choices and places to go for more information.

Colleges and Universities

Several books list all the accredited colleges in the United States and describe the training they offer.

The American Council on Education's publication *American Universities and Colleges* offers practical advice on colleges.

Barron's Guide to the Two-Year College, by Seymour Eskaw, lists technical and vocational institutes as well as junior and community colleges.

For a complete description of schools and course offerings, both academic and vocational, traditional and new, in the classroom and through the mail, for credit or noncredit, look for the book called *The New York Times Guide to Continuing Education in America,* prepared by the College Entrance Examination Board.

Scholarship Information

College expenses are so high, it's a good idea to explore some sources of scholarships available. The financial aid office of the college of your choice will send you a free pamphlet on request. Ask about government and private grants, scholarships, loans, and work-study programs. *A Student's Guide to Five Federal Financial Aid Programs,* a free pamphlet, may be obtained from:

> BEOG (Basic Educational Opportunity Grant)
> Box 84
> Washington, D.C. 20024

Call 1-800-638-6700 for information on what's available. Call 1-800-553-6350 for information and assistance in processing your application. Both numbers are toll free.

Meeting College Costs, also free, is available from:

> College Entrance Examination Board
> 888 Seventh Avenue
> New York, N.Y. 10019

Getting Credit for What You Already Know

There are exams that give you college credit or advanced placement without formal classroom study. These are the College Proficiency Examinations (CPE) and the College-Level Examination Program (CLEP). These general examinations show that your knowledge of a subject equals that of a student who has completed required freshman and sophomore courses. Participating colleges decide how much credit to give and the scores students need to receive the credit. More than two hundred institutions in New York and other northeastern states grant credit through CPE. More than thirteen hundred colleges throughout the country award credit through CLEP.

These exams can cut college expenses. Some people have been given up to a full year's credit after taking them. For information regarding CPE write:

Dr. Donald J. Nolan, Director
College Proficiency Examination Program
State Education Department
Albany, N.Y. 12224

For information regarding CLEP write to:

College Entrance Examination Board
Box 1821
Princeton, N.J. 08541

or:

College Entrance Examination Board
Box 1025
Berkeley, Ca. 94701

Home Study

It's not necessary to live on or near a campus to further your education. For a list of accredited colleges and universities that offer home-study courses, write for a booklet entitled *Guide to Independent Study:*

National University Extension Association
Suite 360
1 DuPont Circle NW
Washington, D.C. 20036

There is a growing trend to grant degrees with only off-campus study. Syracuse University, Goddard College, the University of Oklahoma, and the University of South Florida already have these programs.

Co-op Colleges

These colleges provide a combination of classroom and actual job training. After one year in the classroom, students spend the next four years alternating semesters between schools and participating business firms. They work at paid jobs in their fields during "work" semesters, then return for a semester in the classroom. This provides money for an education and valuable on-the-job experience.

Co-ops used to be more technical than other colleges, but now many fields of study, such as journalism and drama, are offered. To find out more about these programs write to:

> National Commission for Cooperative Education
> 360 Huntington Avenue
> Boston, Mass. 02115

Internships

Many colleges that do not offer co-op programs do offer something similar, called internship programs. In these programs, the student works part time in his or her field while going to school, and works full time during the summer.

To find out more about these programs, check with your school-counseling center librarian, or write to *Directory of Undergraduate Internships:*

> National Center for Public Service Internship Programs
> 1735 Eye Street NW
> Washington, D.C. 20006

or *National Directory of Summer Internships:*

> Career Planning Office
> Haverford College
> Haverford, Pa. 19041

Vocational Colleges

Many areas that have a community college program also have at least one vocational college that offers training in a wide range of occupations at a very low cost. Call and ask for the school catalog. Just browsing through it will give you dozens of ideas about the kinds of jobs you might want to train for. Also look at the *Annual Vocational School Manual,* available from:

> Chronical Guidance
> Moravia, N.Y. 13118

Another source is *Handbook of Trades and Technical Careers and Training,* available from:

> National Association of Trade and Technical Schools
> 2021 L Street NW
> Washington, D.C. 20036

It's a good idea to check the *Occupational Outlook Handbook* in your library to find out what the job possibilities are in the fields you're interested in.

Commercial Vocational Schools

The first question to ask in deciding on a vocational school is, Do I really have to spend all this money? Local community colleges and schools offering adult-education programs do not advertise as much as commercial vocational schools, but they often offer the same courses at much lower tuition fees. Check these out first.

Similarly, some companies offer training programs at their expense. Find out about these by calling the larger companies in your area.

Often, a diploma from a commercial vocational school is not enough to land the job you're after. You may also have to pass a civil-service exam, for example, or become a member of a union. Before you sign up to spend your money, *ask enough questions* to be sure you have all the information you need to make a good decision.

Many vocational schools advertise that they are approved and accredited, but this doesn't assure you of a quality education. Approval by the state and by some national accrediting associations can be routine. In other words, you must check on your own.

One of the best ways to find information about a particular school is to talk with at least three companies that would normally hire the school's graduates. You can find these companies in the Yellow Pages of your phone book under the subject in which you plan to get your training.

Ask the personnel directors about the school and whether they would hire its graduates. If they would, would it be *because* the graduates had been trained by that *particular* vocational school? Ask also if training by that school would make any difference in the starting salary.

If the companies won't answer these questions, ask for their general impressions of the school.

Government Training Programs

Our government offers an abundance of job-training programs and opportunities. There are so many, with changes and additions being made so frequently, that a list of them would be out of date as soon as it was published. The best way to find what is available is to contact one of the following:

- Federal Job Information Center: See the white pages of your telephone book under "United States Government."
- United States Department of Labor, Bureau of Apprenticeships and Training: See the white pages under "United States Government."
- Civil-Service training program: See the white pages under "United States Government." This program opens once a year, in August.
- State Department of Labor employment service: See the white pages under your state's name.

If you already know what you're interested in, a telephone call or visit will tell you what training is available. It's possible, however, that you don't know *what* you really want. In that case, tell the person you talk to about your educational and work background and *ask* him or her to suggest the various training programs you might be able to get into. Your state employment agency can help guide and direct you when you're not quite sure of how to proceed.

Don't get discouraged after a few phone calls. Try different agencies, and you can be sure that at least one of them will have a program that is suitable for you. If the first one can't help, ask the agent to recommend an agency that can. Don't give up!

Industry Training Programs

Many large and medium-sized companies have their own formal training programs, sometimes on their own premises, sometimes in conjunction with local schools or colleges. Formal industry training programs are of two types:

- Management training programs: These are often offered by businesses such as convenience markets and fast-food chains. They combine on-the-job experience with correspondence or classroom courses in order to train you to manage a store or restaurant. More often than not, this type of program will require that you be willing to work at any location to which they assign you, so transportation problems or even a move could be in your future.

A management-training program in a large industry usually chooses only the brightest of the young employees, and spends thousands of dollars in both formal education and interdepartmental training to groom them for upper management. Most employees picked for this program will already have college degrees.

- Skill training programs: These programs are conducted by large manufacturing firms that can't get enough qualified and skilled people. They set up programs to train workers in the skills they need to become machinists, for instance, or assemblers. Then they hire and pay people to learn those skills. Look in the white pages of the phone book under the name of each large company in your area. Call and ask to be put on the waiting lists of companies that do have these programs.
- On-the-job training: Many firms that do not offer formal training programs are nevertheless equipped to give adequate on-the-job training. They understand that many of their young new employees have not been trained for a specific job, and expect to give guidance and close supervision until employees have had a chance to catch on to their new responsibilities. Call the company personnel departments and see.

2 | Getting the Job

The time will come when no matter how much training you have or don't have, actually getting a job becomes the only thing that's really important.

The time-honored way, of course, is to hit the pavement and walk or drive to every business establishment within a ten- or fifteen-mile radius. After doing this for a while, you may begin to think that all employers want the same thing: an eighteen-year-old with twenty years' experience. If you're lucky, you'll wear out only two pairs of shoes or one set of tires before you find a job.

This chapter is dedicated to the proposition that there is an easier way to *get* a job—and to get the *kind* of job you really want and enjoy. Socrates once said that those who work for a living doing something they do not enjoy are engaging in drudgery—no matter how much they are paid for it.

EVALUATING YOUR SKILLS

Starting right can make job hunting a lot easier, and starting right means evaluating your own skills. This may sound like a tough task. Perhaps you think you don't really have any skills. But put yourself in the prospective employers' place for a moment. They know they will have to train you. Basically, they need to know that you're trainable—in other words, that you're interested, alert, and can learn. They'll look for some or all of the following:

- Initiative, ability to be a "self-starter"
- Ability to recognize and solve problems
- Communication skills, ability to write and speak clearly
- Mathematical skills, ability to work with numbers
- Organizational skills, with things, with people, or both
- Ability to accept responsibility
- Technical and practical skills, such as typing, bookkeeping, carpentry, or knowledge of a foreign language

Here are some samples of things that will help convince employers that you're the kind of person they want:

- I had a paper route for four years.
- I was an assistant Girl Scout leader.
- I organized a food and clothing drive at school.
- I tutored history for eighth-graders.
- I did volunteer work at a hospital.
- I created a filing system for the school band.
- I built my own sailboat.
- I visited a senior-citizen home every Wednesday.
- I gave music lessons.
- I taught Sunday School classes.
- I was a teacher's assistant.
- I worked at a fast-food place and was trusted to close up on weekend nights.
- I earned extra cash by setting up a lawn-care service.
- I was a member of the student government at school.

All of these indicate that you do indeed have basic skills, the kind that make you valuable wherever you are. And an employer needs to know this.

SOURCES OF JOB INFORMATION

After evaluating your skills, look at the help-wanted ads in your local newspaper. This should convince you that many employers are looking for people just as eagerly as you're looking for a job. Yet many jobs, if not most, never show up in the newspaper. Small shops put signs in their windows. Large industries often expect people to come in to fill out applications. Many companies, both small and large, depend on state employment agencies to send applicants to them. Remember, when you contact these sources, *ask* if there is anything available that you might be qualified for. Here are ways to get leads:

- Relatives, friends, and neighbors: Let them know you are looking.
- High school or college placement offices: These offices offer free placement to their current students or graduates *only*.
- State Department of Labor: Free placement, job guidance, and occupational testing are usually available. Look in the white pages of your telephone book under the name of your state and find the heading for "Employment Offices," or "Job Services" under "Department of Labor."
- Federal Job Information Center or Job Services: Their services are free. Anyone who works for the United States Government (except military personnel) is called a civil servant and is hired by the United States Civil Service. The Civil Service maintains Federal Job Information Centers throughout the country. Look in the white pages under "United States Government."
- Industrial and crafts shops: Check the Yellow Pages of your phone book for the names of companies that hire people with your training or interest. For example, check under "electronics," "machine shops," or "department stores." Out-of-state directories are available at your local telephone office and some libraries and airports.
- Private employment agencies: Try to avoid using these agencies unless the fee is paid by the employer. They can be expensive. Before you sign any contracts with a private employment agency, make sure you understand *all* the conditions. Discuss them with someone you trust.

SUMMER JOBS

Summer jobs are always scarce, so it pays to apply early. Call the Federal Job Information Center or Job Services Office, listed in the white pages under "United States Government," in early November to get an application for a government summer job.

Some offices and factories hire summer help because many of their employees take vacations then. Apply in January.

Shops and restaurants usually hire summer help. Again, apply early. February or March is about right.

Your local library will have a copy of the *Summer Employ-*

ment Directory of the United States. This directory, published by National Directory Service Incorporated, is issued each November and contains thousands of summer jobs that you can apply for. Your library should also have a copy of *Summer Jobs Directory* and *Summer Employment in Federal Agencies.*

SOCIAL SECURITY NUMBER

In order to get any job, you must have a Social Security number. This nine-digit number is issued to you by the United States Government and is yours for life. The government uses this number to keep track of your earnings for retirement and disability insurance as well as for income tax purposes. Over the years, Social Security numbers have come to be used as sources of identification in the business and educational worlds. It's a good idea to memorize yours, as you will need it often.

When I was younger, it was easy to get a Social Security number. But people who were trying to change their identities abused this system, and now you must meet several requirements before the government will issue a Social Security number. The law requires that you:

- Apply in person if you are eighteen or older, or with your parent if you are under eighteen.
- Furnish evidence of age, identity, and citizenship. Original copies are required.

To furnish evidence of age and citizenship, you will need your original birth certificate or a baptismal certificate recorded before your fifth birthday. Evidence of identity should include at least two of the following types of identification: driver's license, school IDs, voter's registration card, library card, report cards, or similar records.

Before you apply for your number, call your local Social Security office and ask what steps to take. If there is no office near you, call the toll-free information number 1-800-555-1212 and get the toll-free phone number for Social Security in your area.

Check your Social Security record every three years or so to make sure your earnings are being correctly reported on your government record. You can get a free postcard form at any Social Security office for this purpose or request that it be mailed to you. A woman must change her name on her Social Security card when she marries, unless she files a form with her marriage license stating that she will keep her maiden name.

JOB APPLICATIONS

When employers are deciding whom to call in for interviews, your application is often the only thing they can base their decision on. It's important, therefore, to have well-thought-out applications in their files.

Let's consider a typical application and discuss how to fill it out. Before writing anything, read the application over to see what information is required and how it is to be filled in. Note that it asks you to print or type and to give your employment history by listing your last job first. This format is typical of most applications.

How to Fill Out an Application

Some answers work better on job applications than others. Here are some suggestions:

- In the "wages expected" blank, if you don't know what the going rate is, write "open" or "going rate."
- In the blanks for previous employment, you'll be asked to state the reason why you left. Reasons like "better opportunity," "went back to school," or "moved to another city" are much better than "hated the boss" or "work too hard."
- If some blanks do not apply to you, be sure to indicate that you have read them by writing "N/A" in the blank to indicate "not applicable."
- If there is space for outside interests or other data that might add to your qualifications for the job, as on the sample application on page 17, *be sure* to fill it out. A sincere statement of why you think you could do a good job often makes the difference as to whether or not you'll get it.

When You Fill Out an Application

- Dress neatly. You might be interviewed on the first visit.
- Have enough information with you.
- Have your own pen, preferably black with a fine point.
- If your printing is attractive and clear, use it. If not, ask for permission to take your application home so you can type it.

COMPANY NAME

STREET ADDRESS

| I WILL WORK AN IRREGULAR WORK WEEK |
| YES_____ NO_____ |

APPLICATION FOR EMPLOYMENT

PLEASE PRINT OR TYPE

| NAME | LAST | FIRST | MIDDLE | JOB APPLIED FOR | WAGES EXPECTED |

| ADDRESS | NUMBER | STREET | CITY | STATE OR COUNTRY | ZIP |

| PHONE   AREA CODE & NO | SOCIAL SECURITY NUMBER | | WILL YOU WORK   YES ☐   NIGHT SHIFT? NO ☐   OVERTIME? YES ☐ NO ☐ |

EVER BEEN EMPLOYED BY THIS COMPANY?

| YES ☐ NO ☐ DIVISION | WHEN | KIND OF TRANSPORTATION? OWN CAR ☐   PUBLIC ☐   OTHER ☐ |

EMPLOYMENT RECORD – SHOW LAST JOB FIRST – MUST COVER 5 YEARS INCLUDING PERIODS OF UNEMPLOYMENT

COMPANY NAME	PHONE	DATE LEFT	JOB TITLES & NATURE OF WORK	SUPERVISOR
NUMBER	STREET	START DATE		START PAY RATE
CITY	STATE (OR COUNTRY) ZIP	TOTAL MONTHS	REASON FOR LEAVING	END PAY RATE

COMPANY NAME	PHONE	DATE LEFT	JOB TITLES & NATURE OF WORK	SUPERVISOR
NUMBER	STREET	START DATE		START PAY RATE
CITY	STATE (OR COUNTRY) ZIP	TOTAL MONTHS	REASON FOR LEAVING	END PAY RATE

COMPANY NAME	PHONE	DATE LEFT	JOB TITLES & NATURE OF WORK	SUPERVISOR
NUMBER	STREET	START DATE		START PAY RATE
CITY	STATE (OR COUNTRY) ZIP	TOTAL MONTHS	REASON FOR LEAVING	END PAY RATE

COMPANY NAME	PHONE	DATE LEFT	JOB TITLES & NATURE OF WORK	SUPERVISOR
NUMBER	STREET	START DATE		START PAY RATE
CITY	STATE (OR COUNTRY) ZIP	TOTAL MONTHS	REASON FOR LEAVING	END PAY RATE

COMPANY NAME	PHONE	DATE LEFT	JOB TITLES & NATURE OF WORK	SUPERVISOR
NUMBER	STREET	START DATE		START PAY RATE
CITY	STATE (OR COUNTRY) ZIP	TOTAL MONTHS	REASON FOR LEAVING	END PAY RATE

DO NOT WRITE BELOW THIS LINE – TURN TO REVERSE SIDE AND COMPLETE

ENTRIES BELOW FOR USE BY PERSONNEL DEPT. AFTER HIRE ONLY

PERMANENT NO.	DEPT. NO.	JOB TITLE	JOB CODE	TYPE OF HIRE: NEW ☐ REHIRE ☐ REINSTATE ☐ TEMP ☐
SHIFT ☐ DAYS ☐ SWING ☐ GRAVE (6-1/2 HRS) ☐ GRAVE (8 HRS) START TIME _____		PAY CATEGORY ☐ HOURLY ☐ SALARY – NON EXEMPT ☐ SALARY – EXEMPT
START DATE	REQUISITION NO.	☐ DIRECT ☐ INDIRECT	BASE RATE	PAID RATE
U.S. CITIZEN? ☐ YES ☐ NO	BIRTHPLACE	BIRTH DATE	AGE	MARITAL STATUS ☐ M ☐ S ☐ DV ☐ SEP ☐ W	SEX ☐ MALE ☐ FEMALE
DRIVERS LICENSE: STATE NUMBER	EEOC CODE ☐ C75 ☐ O76 ☐ I77 ☐ N78 ☐ S79	FOR ID CARD EYES _____ HAIR _____
DEPENDENTS	INS. CLASS	PAYROLL ACCT	DIST CODE	SUPERVISOR	EXT	LOCATION

The first page of a typical application form

SCHOOL AND EDUCATION RECORD

SCHOOL NAME	CITY & STATE (OR COUNTRY)	GRADE OR YEARS COMPLETED	MAJOR FIELD OF STUDY		GRADUATED OR DEGREE
GRADE OR HIGH		6 - 7 - 8 - 9 10 - 11 - 12			
COLLEGE, TECHNICAL, TRADE, MILITARY		1 - 2 - 3 - 4 5 - 6			

HONORS, AWARDS & PAPERS PUBLISHED:	G/P AVERAGE

PROFESSIONAL OR TECHNICAL LICENSES HELD:	TYPING SPEED	SHORTHAND SPEED

PERSONAL AND REFERENCES

FRIENDS OR RELATIVES IN OUR EMPLOY			EMERGENCY CONTACT	
NAME	RELATIONSHIP	DEPT.	NAME: (FIRST, LAST)	
			NUMBER & STREET	PHONE
			CITY STATE (OR COUNTRY)	

HAVE YOU EVER BEEN CONVICTED OF A FELONY ☐ YES ☐ NO	IF YES, DISCUSS WITH INTERVIEWER	REFERRED TO THIS COMPANY BY:

U.S. MILITARY SERVICE RECORD

BRANCH AND RANK OR SPECIALTY	ENTRY DATE	DISCHARGE DATE	RESERVE OR DRAFT STATUS

OUTSIDE INTEREST AND OTHER DATA WHICH MIGHT ADD TO YOUR QUALIFICATIONS FOR THE JOB SOUGHT.

_____

_____

_____

_____

_____

PLEASE READ CAREFULLY

I HEREBY CERTIFY, that, to the best of my knowledge and belief, the answers given by me to the foregoing questions, and all statements made by me in this application, are correct. I understand that any false information or consequential omission contained in my application is cause for discharge.

I agree to submit to a physical examination. I understand that _____ Corporation will not release to any person any medical diagnosis which results from said examination. I also authorize all of my former employers, school officials, instructors and persons named herein as references to give to _____ Corporation any information they have regarding me, whether or not such information is on their records. I hereby release said companies and individuals from any liability for any damage whatsoever resulting from the giving of such information.

I understand that in order to avoid unnecessary delay I may be permitted to go to work before all reports are received. If such reports show that I do not meet all standards of _____ Corporation, I agree that my employment may be terminated immediately.

DATE_____ APPLICANT SIGNATURE_____

FOR PERSONNEL DEPARTMENT USE

REFERRED TO:	DATE	MEDICAL STATUS	PHYS. LIMIT. CODE
REFERRED TO:	DATE	MEDICAL SIGNATURE M.D.	DATE
OTHER ACTION		PLANT SECURITY SIGNATURE	DATE
		PAYROLL SIGNATURE	DATE
		PERSONNEL SIGNATURE	DATE

FILE INSTRUCTION: 1 YR ☐   3 YRS ☐

The second page of an application form

Have Important Information with You

To be sure that you can make out the application completely, bring a card or sheet of paper that lists the following:

- Your Social Security number
- Names, addresses, and telephone numbers of previous employers
- Dates of employment and your duties during that period
- Educational history
- Names, addresses, and telephone numbers of your personal references
- A statement indicating your outside interests and willingness to work

This should make it easy to copy your information from the card onto the application, and will make you look resourceful and well organized.

THE RÉSUMÉ

A résumé is a personal fact sheet designed to get a prospective employer's attention. Its objective is to present you in the most favorable light and make the employer anxious to interview you.

Because each of us has different skills, abilities, and objectives, each résumé will be unique. If you are just getting out of high school, you may not need one, but a résumé is essential for a college graduate or anyone with considerable experience.

A résumé should be *no more than one page in length* and should be carefully structured to present your strong points. Neatness counts! Since your résumé is your first introduction to a prospective employer, it should be attractive, neat, and well thought out. Use a late-model electric typewriter or have your résumé professionally typeset. It's worth the investment. There are many ways to organize an effective résumé. One good format is shown on page 20.

Your local library or school-placement service can provide you with many more-detailed books and illustrations of résumés.

YOUR NAME
YOUR ADDRESS
CITY, STATE, ZIP
AREA CODE AND TELEPHONE NUMBER

OBJECTIVE: A brief statement of your job objective

EXPERIENCE: List all job-related experience that shows an employer that you are capable in your chosen field. If you have no job-related work experience, include part-time, summer, or full-time jobs that contributed to your over-all skills. Volunteer work should be included.

EDUCATION: If you have a college degree, list the college, its location, and the year you were graduated. If not, list the number of semesters of college credit you have. If you have none, list your high school, its location, and the year you were graduated.

Mention the major curriculum you studied and any honors or scholarships you received. If you're proud of your grade-point average, include it. If not, forget it. You may list major courses (not more than five) that might impress an employer. List extracurricular activities at which you excelled.

SPECIAL INTERESTS: List the knowledge and special skills you possess that show that you would be a valuable employee. These may or may not be directly related to the job. They may include your hobbies or school activities. For some hints, refer to the skill-evaluation discussion on page 12.

PERSONAL DETAILS: Age, health, marital status, number of children, if any, may be included. Many people believe, however, that such personal data should be omitted.

Do not include race, religion, or your picture in a résumé.

THE COVERING LETTER

If you are mailing your résumé, you will need a different covering letter for each company you apply to. It should be brief (one page at most), and it should state your interest in working for that particular company. Type it on good-quality white paper and address it, if possible, to the person in the company who is responsible for hiring in your field. Better still, address it to the head of the department you are particularly interested in. You can usually get that person's name over the telephone.

In the opening paragraph, give your reason for writing the letter and mention the job or type of work you are interested in. In the second paragraph, state your reasons for wanting to work for that company and for believing your qualifications and skills will make a real contribution. Refer to your résumé in this paragraph.

The final paragraph should suggest a date and time for an interview with the promise of a follow-up telephone call for confirmation of the interview date. Be sure to sign the letter.

THE INTERVIEW

The interview will probably be the deciding factor in whether or not you get the job.

You'll be interviewed by someone who has a lot more experience in interviewing than you have in being interviewed. That person knows this and will therefore try to set you at ease. Basically, the interviewer will be looking for specific job skills, but just as important will be his or her impression of you. Things that will be important are your initiative, honesty, dependability, and enthusiasm. Your qualifications at this point may not be many, but willingness to work and the ability to convey the impression that you will be a hard worker will be helpful.

General Rules to Follow

- Be prompt. Arrive at least ten minutes before the scheduled time of the interview.
- Dress in neat, simple clothes.
- Have a positive attitude.
- *Never* take anyone with you.
- Talk intelligently about the company's products or services and how you think you can help. Ask intelligent questions. If you do some homework on the company or business in advance, this should be easy.
- Mannerisms are important. *Don't* smoke, tap nervously, fidget, slouch in your chair, talk too much, or clam up and say nothing. *Do* shake hands firmly, look the interviewer in the eye, but don't stare, speak in a normal, firm voice, smile, and be attentive. And don't worry. It'll go well.

- Be calm and let the interviewer control the meeting.
- Never criticize your former employer or fellow workers.
- If you are inexperienced, say your salary is open or that you'll accept the established rate.
- Watch for clues that the interview is over. If the employer does not tell you his or her decision right away, ask when you can call.
- Thank the employer.
- If you drive to the interview, park at a long-term meter.

Some Questions You May Be Asked

It's hard to predict what you'll be asked, but here are some frequently asked questions:

- Tell me about yourself.
- What are your hobbies, your outside interests?
- What are your strengths? What are your weaknesses?
- Where do you want to end up in the business?
- What is your training or aptitude for this job?
- Why do you want to work for *this* company?

There are no right or wrong answers for any of these questions, so take time before the interview to think about how you'll answer them if they're asked.

Before going to your first interview, it might be helpful to try a "mock interview." You probably have a friend or relative who would be willing to play the role of the employer. Let one of them read this section and then give you an interview to evaluate your answers, attitude, and mannerisms in a way that will help you in a real situation.

Follow-up

Drop a note to the person who interviewed you. Thank him or her for taking the time to see you and again express your interest in the job and your desire to work for the company.

You may be told that your interview went well, but that "there's just nothing open at this time." Request that your application be kept in the "active file." Don't be timid. Be persistent. Call back about once a week, and tell the person you spoke with that you're still interested and available. Persistence pays off for many people.

STARTING YOUR OWN BUSINESS

There's a word to describe the special people who have the imagination, the flair, and, yes, even the guts to go into business for themselves. The word is *entrepreneur*—and if you're about to become one, here, perhaps, is the best tip you'll ever receive.

An organization of retired owners of small businesses and retired executives of large corporations called the Service Corps of Retired Executives (SCORE) can help you get started and become successful in your own business. Each member of this organization has accumulated a lifetime of practical, down-to-earth experience. They know how to get things done quickly, how to cut red tape, how to avoid expensive mistakes, how to treat all of the problems that can plague *your* business. And the best news is: all of this expensive and valuable consultation is absolutely free!

You'll find SCORE in the white pages of your telephone book, or you can call the Small Business Administration (in the white pages under United States Government) and they will tell you the number of the local SCORE group.

The Small Business Administration (SBA) has many useful *free* booklets. Call the SBA toll-free number, 1-800-433-7212 (Texas 1-800-792-8901).

Some of the more useful booklets are SBA 115A, which lists all *free* SBA publications; MA-4, *How SBA Can Help You Go Into Business;* and OPI-6, *Small Business Loans.*

A third source of information for the independent business person is the National Federation of Independent Business. Write for free information to:

National Federation of Independent Business
150 W. 20th Avenue
San Mateo, Ca. 94403

UNEMPLOYMENT

If you lose your job, apply for unemployment benefits immediately, even though you may get another job soon. Many states base their unemployment benefits on your average income over the previous six months. If you applied after three months of job-hunting, for example, you would receive considerably less in benefits than you would if you had applied immediately. Call your state employment agency for details.

3 | Getting an Apartment

My son Mike has had his own apartment for a number of years. He never seemed to have any major problems, but the same is not true for his brother Ed. When Ed went off to college, he shared an apartment with two friends, and, apparently a limitless number of gremlins. It was a nice place, and even had its own laundromat. And that's where the first gremlin struck. When the boys ran out of laundry detergent, one of them substituted a cup of dishwashing liquid. No bells, no whistles, just mounds and mounds of suds pushed open the door of the washing machine, dropped silently to the floor, and slithered to fill every corner. Score one for the gremlins.

Score two when the guys couldn't see any reason to clean the oven, and the gremlins set fire to it. Trying to remember home-emergency procedures, one of them called the fire department while another threw flour in the oven. Pouf! It burned beautifully. The third ran out and pounded on doors until he found someone with a fire extinguisher. That worked. If they had thrown baking soda on the fire instead of flour, the smoke damage would have been reduced, because the baking soda would have smothered the grease fire.

Round three went to the gremlins too. One day Ed returned from class to find a brand-new swimming pool in the kitchen. The hot-water pipe had let go at the seam! The other guys were trying to dam up the hot water to keep it from getting into the rest of the place because they had no idea where to turn off the main water supply. Luckily, Ed knew where the shutoff was, but I think the kids could have bought the place for the cost of the labor they put into the mopping up operation.

Nevertheless, your first apartment can be exciting. It may be the first time you're on your own, your chance to have things just the way you like them. Look forward to apartment hunting and be excited about it, but beware. If you don't keep some basic hints in mind and take proper precautions, you might be stuck for a year in something you can't afford and don't like. This chapter will give you the data you need to get the best deal the first time.

FINDING LEADS

Besides driving through neighborhoods, looking for rental signs, apartment hunters can explore five major sources of information:

- Friends may be your best means of finding out about available apartments.
- Newspaper rental ads will give you an idea of what's available and the cost. Apartments in the classified section of your newspaper are usually listed under both "furnished" and "unfurnished." In big cities they will be listed by areas also.
- Real estate agents carry lists of rentals in their areas. If you call an agent and find an apartment through him or her, the landlord pays the fee.
- Apartment finders are businesses that charge you a fee. Most of their listings come from the newspapers, so try to avoid this service, as it can be costly.
- Apartment managers are helpful if you know of apartments where you would like to live. Go direct to the building manager. If nothing is available, leave your name and phone number, and ask the manager to call you if an apartment is vacated.

WHAT TO LOOK FOR

No apartment is perfect, but all apartments should be clean and well cared for. The following check list will help you find livable quarters. The more you can check off, the happier you'll be after you move in.

- Try not to be on a noisy street, although the higher up you are the less street noise you hear.

- Check for good light and ventilation.
- Make sure there are adequate fire exits or escapes.
- Check the size and number of closets.
- Try to find an apartment that is close to public transportation and shopping.
- Make sure the apartment has hot and cold water, that the toilet and shower work well, and that there are no leaky faucets.
- Determine that all the electrical outlets work. Take along a small night light to check outlets.
- Check the lighting in the entrance, hallways, and parking lots to insure safety at night. Find out if there is an intercom system.
- See that the windows move up and down smoothly.
- Check the locks on the windows and on all the entry doors. They should be solid. Deadbolts on the doors are excellent. It may be advisable to install your own lock, to which no former tenants have the key, when you move in.
- Find out whether there is a superintendent, and who is responsible for repairs.
- Check to see if the stove, refrigerator, air conditioner, and any other appliances work.
- Bring along a measuring tape to determine whether your furniture will fit.
- Check the apartment for sound. It should be as close to soundproof as possible.
- Determine whether the building has laundry facilities, which would be very desirable.
- Note whether the apartment has electric or some other form of heat, and find out if you'll have to pay for it. This can make a big difference in the over-all cost of the apartment.
- Try to talk to one of the other tenants in the building before you see the manager. He or she will usually tell you what it's like to live there.
- Check that there are parking places if you have a car.
- If you drive to work, try to live east of the firm, so you won't drive into the sun going to and from your job.

NEGOTIATING FOR AN APARTMENT

When you look for an apartment, try to make a good impression by appearing both neat and knowledgeable. Many landlords will ask you to fill out an application form. Be sure to leave no blank spaces. Some landlords will ask for an application fee that in effect holds the apartment for you for a limited time. Find out whether you get the money back if you decide not to rent, and whether it is applied to your first month's rent. Be sure you really want the apartment before you put any money down. You may want the apartment only if the landlord is willing to make certain repairs, such as plastering or painting. Make a list of required repairs when you look at the apartment. Whatever the arrangement, be sure to get it in writing. Another important question to ask is how long it takes to find out whether your application has been accepted.

Rental Agreements

You can rent on a month-to-month basis, or lease the apartment for a year or more. Be sure to get all agreements in writing. A lease gives you more protection but requires a long-term commitment on your part. With a lease, you are assured that you can stay in the apartment for the time limit agreed on, usually a year. The landlord may not raise the rent during that period unless the lease allows it. In a month-to-month agreement, the landlord may evict you or raise the rent under certain conditions. Normally a lease will include the following details:

- Description of the dwelling
- Length of time lease will run
- Names of landlord and tenant
- Date on which the rent is due
- Amount of rent and any "late charges"
- Who is responsible for maintenance
- Who pays for utilities (gas, electric, heat, water)
- How much notice is necessary to end lease
- Landlord's rules and regulations

Before You Sign the Lease
- Read and *understand* it.
- Remember that no lease is legal until it is signed by both parties.
- Leave no blank spaces in the contract.
- Ask the landlord to write out all oral promises, such as what

repairs he will make before you move in, and have him sign the agreement.

- Choose roommates carefully. If more than one person signs the lease and everyone else moves out, the landlord can hold you responsible to meet the terms of the lease.
- Get the landlord's telephone number and address, in case you need to contact him.
- Find out what deposits are necessary and how they are refunded.

Deposits

When you sign the rental agreement, you will probably be asked for a deposit, usually in an amount equal to one month's rent. Find out the exact purpose of the deposit and the circumstances under which it will be refunded. *Keep* receipts for all deposits. You'll need them when you move out.

If your deposit is not returned within two weeks of your leaving the apartment, contact your landlord in writing (certified letter) to learn the reason for the delay. If the problem can't be resolved, you can take the landlord to Small Claims Court. If the court finds that the landlord is trying to cheat you, you may be awarded punitive damages as well as your deposit. The amount of punitive damages varies from state to state.

The following are the types and purposes of deposits usually required:

- Cleaning deposits allow the landlord to clean or paint the apartment *after* you leave. Normally, the landlord can keep *only* the part of the deposit necessary to clean or paint the apartment.
- Damage deposits must be refunded when you leave, unless you caused damage beyond normal wear and tear or failed to give adequate written notice before moving. If you do more damage than the deposit will cover, the landlord can take you to court to get more money. To avoid any hassle over the damage deposit, check the apartment before you move in and list damages caused by the previous tenants. Then date it and ask the landlord to sign it. Keep this record and your copy of the lease with your important papers. When you're ready to move out, try to get your landlord to make a damage inspection with you and return your damage deposit on the spot.

- Security deposits are sometimes used instead of damage deposits. The catch is that although the damage deposit must be refunded, the security deposit does not have to be refunded unless you rent the apartment for a certain length of time, which should be specified in writing.

BEING A GOOD TENANT

The United States Department of Housing and Urban Development has some good suggestions for apartment dwellers:

- Be businesslike in your dealings with the landlord.
- Report all problems.
- Put all your communications in writing.
- Keep a copy of all written communications and receipts.
- Pay your rent and utilities on time.
- Be a good neighbor (considerate of others).
- Keep your apartment clean.
- Before moving out, give the landlord written notice at least one month in advance or by the time agreed upon in the lease.
- Leave the apartment clean.
- When you move, send change-of-address cards to friends and others who send you mail.

YOUR BASIC RIGHTS

Be aware that problems *can* come up when you rent an apartment. It's wise to know your rights and how to get help if you need it. When you rent, you have a right to a livable apartment. This means plumbing and lights that work, doors and windows that lock, heating and cooling systems (if they're included in the lease) that are in operating condition. As a renter, you also have the right to privacy. This means that the landlord may not waltz into your apartment anytime he chooses, without your consent. You can't keep him out in all circumstances, however. State laws vary, but you cannot unreasonably withhold consent from the landlord to enter your apartment in order to inspect it, to make necessary repairs or alterations, to show it to a prospective buyer, or in an emergency. In all cases but those of emergency, the landlord should schedule any necessary entry about twenty-four hours in advance, and at a time that is convenient for you.

Illegal Leases

While the majority of landlords are fair, some may try to take advantage of you. There may be provisions in leases that are illegal, but remember your signing a lease doesn't make them legal. Some examples of these illegal provisions are:

- Any provision that says you will accept blame in any future dispute with your landlord or pay the landlord's legal fees in that dispute.
- Any provision permitting the landlord to take possession of your personal property if you can't pay the rent.
- Any provision permitting the landlord to retaliate against you by eviction, shutting off the water, or any means if you complain to the proper authorities about living conditions or try to organize a tenants' group.

Code Violations

If your apartment is in general disrepair, and the landlord won't do anything about it, see if he's in violation of the housing code. A housing code is a list of building regulations that provide for the safe and healthy living conditions that all rentals are required to meet (no broken plumbing, leaky roof, and the like). However, housing codes are not always enforced. In fact, one government study showed that 60 percent of the communities in the United States did not enforce these codes. Call your city hall and ask to talk to someone in the Office of Housing. Ask what the codes are and whether they are enforced. If they can't help you, call any of the following:

- Consumer protection agency
- Tenant organization
- Attorney general's office
- Call for Action
- City or county health department (if your landlord threatens to shut off your water)

GIVING NOTICE

When you do decide to move, you must notify your landlord in writing thirty days in advance, even if you have a lease, or your landlord can keep your deposit.

Here's a good sample of a letter terminating a lease:

> Your Address
> City, State, Zip Code
> Date

Name of Leaseholder
City, State

Dear Sir:

As required by the terms of my lease, I am notifying you that I will vacate the premises and terminate the lease no later than (day, month, year).

Please arrange for any necessary inspections prior to that date and arrange to refund my deposit(s) (amount) at that time.

> Sincerely,
> Your name

MOVING

Of course you'll want to plan your move before you give notice. Just the thought of moving depresses some of us for weeks, but if you organize in advance you'll survive.

Think through a move before you have to leave your present quarters. Here are some general preparations:

- Call the telephone, electric, gas, and water companies (if they are in your name), and arrange to have your services stopped at one address and started at the new address.
- Send change-of-address cards to: magazines, newspapers, friends, businesses where you have charge accounts, the local post office, your school, office, bank, insurance agent, doctor, dentist, automobile registrar, and driver's license bureau.

Do-It-Yourself Moving

To cut costs and be sure that your possessions will receive the best care, it is often wise to move on your own. This requires energy, muscle power, people to help you, and loads of preparation. Here's the sequence:

- Arrange for the truck or trailer in advance.
- Think about buying insurance that will cover personal and

property damage. Most companies that rent equipment to do-it-yourself movers offer this insurance.

- Arrange to rent dollies (little platforms on wheels) and pads to protect your furniture. Some trucks have hydraulic lifts, which really help.
- Make sure the friends who plan to help know the exact date of your move.
- Discard all the things you no longer want or have a garage sale.
- On each packing box, write the contents and the room each box goes in at the new address.
- Take important papers and jewelry with you.
- Pack a lunch in advance, and if it is going to be a long move prepare an easy dinner. Lots of snacks and drinks help too.
- Have one person guard the truck at all times if there's a possibility of theft.
- Pack one box with a change of clothes, linens, toilet articles, alarm clock, and enough dishes, soap, toilet paper, light bulbs, and pans to last you until you finish unpacking.
- Return your rented equipment as soon as possible to avoid extra charges.

Professional Moving

If you plan to use a moving company, call the Interstate Commerce Commission (ICC, in the white pages under "United States Government") and obtain their informative booklet, "Summary of Information for Shippers of Household Goods," and ask for the annual performance report of the twenty largest interstate movers. If you are interested in the performance record of any of the hundreds of other authorized interstate movers, phone the toll-free number 1-800-424-9312. This information will help you decide which movers to call for estimates. When an interstate moving company solicits your business or gives you an estimate, it is required to furnish you with a copy of the full report it has filed with the ICC on its service performance during the preceding year.

Each state has its own regulations concerning movers. Check with your local consumer-protection agency to find out more about the rules in your state. On moves within the state, you are usually charged an hourly rate for less than 50 miles or a mileage and weight rate for distances over 50 miles.

The rates of both interstate and within-state movers cover loading, travel, and unloading only. Additional services, such as packing and unpacking, cost extra, and you should fully understand the cost of any service before you authorize it.

The insurance included in your rate is based on the weight of each item, not on its value. Anything of real value should be covered by additional insurance. Be sure to ask your movers to explain their insurance program fully. As a precaution, make sure all your packing boxes are closed and sealed both before and after the move.

SETTING UP AN APARTMENT

Now that you've found and arranged to move into the best apartment within your budget, you'll want to outfit it. Here are some considerations that it make it a lot easier.

Utilities and Telephone

Before moving in, notify the gas, electric, and telephone companies. Each of these utilities has a large back order of tasks to accomplish, and needs all the time you can give it to schedule its service.

Each utility will want a deposit, normally about fifty dollars. If you are moving from another location served by the same utility and have already made a deposit in the other location, you won't have to pay again. Also, if you last lived with your parents and they are willing to guarantee payment of the utilities, you should be able to negotiate a no-deposit agreement.

For future reference, make sure the landlord tells you where to find the main water shutoff, the fuse box or circuit-breaker box, and the main gas shutoff. Murphy's Law says that if anything can go wrong, it will, and at the worst possible time, so you may save yourself a lot of grief by knowing how to shut off your own utilities in an emergency. Most toilets and many sinks have small water shutoff valves beneath them, so you won't have to shut off the main water supply when making small repairs. Also make sure you get two keys so that you can leave one with someone you trust if you lock yourself out. You might leave an extra car key with your friend too.

Furnishings

You can spend a lot or a little to make your apartment livable, and there are ways to save money.

What you need in the way of tables, chairs, sofas, beds, dressers, and other major furniture depends on your taste, your budget, and the size of your apartment. You'll be able to buy whatever you decide on at bargain prices at a second-hand furniture store. The cheapest, and often the best, of these are the Salvation Army, Goodwill Industries, and the St. Vincent de Paul stores. These are listed in your Yellow Pages under "Furniture, Used," or "Second Hand Stores." They deliver for a small fee. Once you've begun to accumulate furnishings, it may be wise to consider purchasing renter's homeowner insurance (see Chapter 7).

You will need a great deal more besides furniture. Many of the items on the following lists can be bought cheaply. You can pick and choose from these lists. I've tried to give you practical minimums for comfortable living.

KITCHEN UTENSILS

Really Need	*Nice to Have*
frying pan	cookbook (check library)
sauce pan	large fork and spoon
spatula	measuring cup
can opener	plastic dishpan and drainer
pot holder	paring knife
sink stopper	scouring pad
sharp knife	vegetable peeler
mixing bowl	cheese slicer
glass	paper towels, napkins
cup	plastic and aluminum wrap
plate	facial tissues
bowl	hammer
fork	pliers, screwdriver
knife	nails, screws
spoon	picture hangers
sponge	additional dishes
dishwashing detergent	additional silverware
garbage can, garbage bags	

The first time you go shopping, it'll be expensive, but many of the things you buy (or borrow from your parents) will stay on your shelves for months.

KITCHEN SUPPLIES

salt and pepper
butter
coffee or tea
eggs
milk
bread
sugar or honey
cooking oil
catsup, mustard
bouillon cubes
mayonnaise
potatoes
onions (dried or fresh)

seasonings
macaroni
spaghetti
canned or dried beans
canned vegetables
canned fruits
peanut butter
jelly or jam
meats, luncheon meat, fish
vegetables
dairy products
baking soda

BATHROOM SUPPLIES

cosmetics, cream
bath soap
toilet paper
facial tissue
talcum powder
tweezers
razor, blades
two face cloths
two towels
shampoo
toothbrush, toothpaste

deodorant
nail clippers
comb, brush
toilet-bowl brush
scouring powder
sponge
rags
tile cleaner
wastebasket
cup

FIRST AID

aspirin
Band-Aids
antacid
Vaseline

gauze
adhesive tape
antibiotic ointment
alcohol

BEDROOM SUPPLIES

two sheets
two pillow cases

pillow
blanket

BEDROOM SUPPLIES
plastic bag or hamper   clothes brush
alarm clock   clothes hangers
shoe polish

MISCELLANEOUS SUPPLIES
rags   ironing board
light bulbs   pens, pencils, paper
needle and thread   cellophane tape
scissors   laundry soap, bleach
flashlight   broom, dustpan
candles   string
pins   mop, bucket
calendar   electric fuses
iron

Helpful Hints

• Reserve a place next to the door you use to go out. (Our place is a small hall table.) Make it a practice to put anything you should take with you in that spot. Use it for keys, letters to be mailed, sunglasses, school or work papers, and so on. Within a few days it becomes second nature to check that spot every time you leave. It's surprising how few things you forget and how many frustrations you avoid.

• Reserve a drawer in the kitchen, a desk, or anywhere, into which you can stuff anything you think is important, like receipts, warranties, and anything else that looks as though you could need it later. When you're sitting around on a rainy weekend afternoon, sort through what's piled up in your drawer and file it in your permanent file. We use a couple of accordion envelopes that we found in a variety store for this purpose.

• Your apartment won't be complete without a telephone list. Make a copy like this one and tape it near the phone or attach it to your refrigerator with a magnet.

FRIENDS AND RELATIVES
Mom and and Dad
Jeanne
Pete

work

bank

checking-account number

savings-account number

insurance agent

electric company

gas company

telephone company

EMERGENCY NUMBERS

rescue squad

emergency ambulance

hospital emergency

fire department

police department

crime prevention

poison control

doctor

dentist

health clinic

drugstore

- Get a cookbook that defines terms like "scald," "score," "sauté," and others. Here are some other things you might want to know:

tsp = t = teaspoon
tbl = T = tablespoon
cup = c = 8 ounces
3 teaspoons = 3t = 1 tablespoon = 1T
4 tablespoons = 4T = ¼ cup
1 cup = 8 fluid ounces
2 cups = 1 pint
4 cups = 1 quart
4 quarts = 1 gallon
1 stick of butter = ½ cup of butter
juice of 1 lemon = 3 tablespoons
1 medium onion (chopped) = ½ cup onion
1 pound of fresh mushrooms = 6 to 8 ounces of canned mushrooms
8 ounces of *un*cooked spaghetti = 5 cups of cooked
1 cup of *un*cooked rice = 2 cups of cooked rice
1 pound of nuts = 2 cups of nut meats
1 ounce of chocolate = ¼ cup of cocoa
1 tablespoon of fresh herbs = 1 teaspoon of dried herbs
1 clove of garlic = 1 *section* of a whole garlic bulb
1 medium clove of garlic = ⅛ teaspoon dried garlic

4 | Managing Money

So many fine books on personal finances and money management are stacked on the shelves of your local library that I won't even try to be comprehensive in this chapter. But I would like to pass on some practical money-saving tips I've picked up over a lifetime of being frugal.

BUDGETS

It's easier to manage your finances if you know how much money you must allocate for each major expense. Your librarian can recommend good books on budgeting and personal finances, but here is a general budget based on your average monthly salary. Consumer Credit Counseling suggests these guidelines for budgeting your *take-home* pay:

Expenses	Percentage of Salary
Housing	25–30%
Food	20–25%
Transportation	10%
Credit payments	10%
Clothing	5%
Medical	5%
Recreation	5%
Savings	5%
Miscellaneous	5%

Here is how your personal budget might look:

Item	Estimated Expenses	Amount Spent
Rent	_____	_____
Gas	_____	_____
Electricity	_____	_____
Water	_____	_____
Telephone	_____	_____
Insurance	_____	_____
Monthly loan Payments:		
Car	_____	_____
Others	_____	_____
Groceries	_____	_____
Clothing	_____	_____
Doctor and dentist	_____	_____
Medicines	_____	_____
Automobile or transportation	_____	_____
Oil and gasoline	_____	_____
Laundry	_____	_____
Charity and church	_____	_____
Entertainment	_____	_____
Daily expenses	_____	_____
Others	_____	_____
Savings	_____	_____

Total take-home pay	_____
Total expenses	_____
Extra	_____

To set up your monthly budget, fill in fixed monthly payments, such as rent, car payments, and insurance. Then fill in your best estimates of the costs of the other items. Add the figures in the estimated-expenses column and see if your take-home pay covers your expenses. You may have to pare down.

At the end of your first month on the budget, fill in the actual amounts spent and see how well you have done. Adjustments may be needed to make the budget fit your spending patterns and the money available.

FINANCIAL RECORDS

Do you need to keep every scrap of paper that has a number on it? By no means! Yet some records can be very valuable, and it's a good idea to keep them in a safe place. I use an accordion folder, but any shoebox or large envelope would do. My folder holds my *current records,* such as bills, receipts for cash payments, and canceled checks. I also have an inexpensive metal box for my *permanent records.* These include:

- Birth certificates
- Auto titles
- Warranties
- Lease agreements
- Insurance policies
- W-2 forms, income-tax records

I also have two cards, one for my wallet and one for my permanent-record box, a 5-by-8-inch card that looks like this:

Social Security number _____

Name of bank _____

Checking account number _____

Savings account number _____

Auto insurance company _____

Policy number _____

Agent's name _____

Phone number _____

Health insurance company _____

Policy number _____

Agent's name _____

Phone number _____

Life insurance company _____

Policy number _____

Agent's name _____

Phone number _____

Credit cards	Card number	Phone for lost card
_____	_____	_____
_____	_____	_____
_____	_____	_____

Notify in emergency _____ Phone _____

The card I keep in my wallet has been cut down to the correct size and provides vital information in emergency situations:

```
My name            _____
Address          _____
Phone            _____
Blood type       _____
Allergic reactions       _____
Notify in emergency      _____
Phone            _____
```

INCOME TAXES

Many may think I am strange, but I don't mind paying income taxes—not when I stop to consider the hundreds of government services from which I, personally, benefit.

Anyone who earns a designated minimum income over the course of the year must file a federal income-tax return by April 15 of the following year. Depending on where you live, you may be required to file a state or a city income-tax return as well. In this section I will discuss federal tax forms only.

The federal income-tax forms (W-2, W-4, and 1040A) and the federal tax table used in this section may vary slightly from year to year. Obtain copies of the latest forms and the booklets explaining how to file them from your local Internal Revenue Service (IRS) office (listed in the white pages of your phone book under "United States Government"), from your bank, or from your post office.

How to Get the Smallest Amount Withheld from Your Paycheck

The federal income-tax system operates on a "pay as you go" basis. Employers must withhold income-tax money from all of their employees' pay checks. The amount withheld is determined by the amount of money you are paid and the number of allowances or dependents you claim on your W-4 form. The total amount withheld each year is designed by IRS to equal the amount you will probably owe that year.

Too much tax is withheld from the salaries of many young people, because they don't know about the special allowances they can use, such as *special withholding* and *exemption from withholding.*

Special Withholding Allowance

Each time you begin to work with a new employer, you will be asked to fill out and file with your employer an "Employee's Withholding Allowance Certificate," better known as a W-4 form. If you are single, you will usually have only one dependent—yourself. But if you are a single person with only one employer, or a married person who has only one employer and whose spouse is not employed, you can claim a special withholding allowance plus your own exemption, and are therefore entitled to two allowances on your W-4 form (see example). This will give you more take-home pay in your check.

Exemptions from Withholding

If you didn't pay taxes last year and do not expect to earn enough to have to pay taxes this year, you may use your W-4 form to claim "exemption" from withholding tax. This means that your employers will *not* deduct federal income taxes from your pay check. They will continue to deduct Social Security (FICA) and local taxes if applicable.

Students and part-time workers who will not earn over $3,300 a year (amount subject to change annually) should claim exemption as instructed on line 3 of the W-4 form. This means no federal taxes will be withheld and you won't have to file an income-tax return to claim a refund.

The Record of Your Taxes: W-2 Form

In order to file your income-tax return, you will need a W-2 form from your employers. They are required by law to send you a "Wage and Tax Statement (W-2 form)" by January 31 of the year following your employment. The W-2 form is a record of the wages you were paid, the wages that were subject to income-tax withholding, and the amount of federal income tax withheld. It also shows the amount of Social Security (FICA) tax withheld. This Social Security tax (FICA) is not refundable.

Employee's Withholding Allowance Certificate

(Use for Wages Paid After December 31, 1978)

This certificate is for income tax withholding purposes only. It will remain in effect until you change it. If you claim exemption from withholding, you will have to file a new certificate on or before April 30 of next year.

Type or print your full name

John Smith

Your social security number

439-18-7253

Home address (number and street or rural route)

15 Cypress Road

Marital Status

[X] Single [ ] Married

[ ] Married, but withhold at higher Single rate

Note: If married, but legally separated, or spouse is a nonresident alien, check the single block.

City or town, State, and ZIP code

Any Town, U.S.A

1 Total number of allowances you are claiming   2

2 Additional amount, if any, you want deducted from each pay (if your employer agrees) . . . . $

3 I claim exemption from withholding (see instructions). Enter "Exempt" . . . .

Under the penalties of perjury, I certify that the number of withholding allowances claimed on this certificate does not exceed the number to which I am entitled. If claiming exemption from withholding, I certify that I incurred no liability for Federal income tax for last year and I anticipate that I will incur no liability for Federal income tax for this year.

Signature ► John Smith   Date ► Feb 26 , 19 79

This W-4 form shows your own exemption plus a special withholding allowance.

1 Total number of allowances you are claiming . . . .

2 Additional amount, if any, you want deducted from each pay (if your employer agrees) . . . . $

3 I claim exemption from withholding (see instructions). Enter "Exempt" . . . . Exempt

Under the penalties of perjury, I certify that the number of withholding allowances claimed on this certificate does not exceed the number to which I am entitled. If claiming exemption from withholding, I certify that I incurred no liability for Federal income tax for last year and I anticipate that I will incur no liability for Federal income tax for this year.

Signature ► John Smith   Date ► July 8 , 19 79

Claim "exempt" on line 3 of your W-4 form if you expect to earn less than $3,300.00 a year.

1 Control number 22222	2 Employer's State number			
3 Employer's name, address, and ZIP code Green's Grocery 15 Plain St Anytown, USA, 12345	4 Subtotal [ ] Correction [ ] Void [ ]			
	5 Employer's identification number 48-0263721			
	6 Advance EIC payment		7	
8 Employee's social security number 631-18-7284	9 Federal income tax withheld $324.17	10 Wages, tips, other compensation $2380.00	11 FICA tax withheld $136.13	12 Total FICA wages $2380.00
13 Employee's name (first, middle, last) Mary P. White	14 Pension plan coverage? Yes/No No	15	16 FICA tips	
51 Hope Ln Anytown, USA 12345	18 State income tax withheld —	19 State wages, tips, etc. —	20 Name of State	
	21 Local income tax withheld —	22 Local wages, tips, etc. —	23 Name of locality	
17 Employee's address and ZIP code				

Form W-2 Wage and Tax Statement 1979

Copy B To be filed with employee's **FEDERAL** tax return
This information is being furnished to the Internal Revenue Service.

Department of the Treasury — Internal Revenue Service

The company you work for issues the W-2 form at about the end of January.

If you file a return, attach Copy B of your W-2 with your return. Your employers send Copy A to the Social Security Administration and keep Copy D for their records. Keep Copy C for your records. In some states additional copies are provided to be filed with your state and local income tax.

See the sample of Copy B of a W-2 form, which is the one you send in when you file your income tax, on page 43.

If you fail to receive a W-2 form by January 31 or receive an incorrect W-2, contact your local IRS (Internal Revenue Service) office. They will help you with problems.

Who Must File a Tax Return

Every year the government issues a chart showing the minimum amount of income you must receive to file an income-tax return. Your employers should know this amount, so ask them, or call your local IRS office or Federal Information Center. If you earned less than that amount, and no tax was withheld because you claimed "exemption" on your W-4 form, you need not file a return. If you didn't claim "exemption" on the W-4 form, you are entitled to a refund and must file a tax return to receive it.

Filing for a Refund When You've Made Less Than the Minimum Taxable Income

You earned $2,380.00 in 1979 (less than the minimum taxable income), and $324.17 was withheld from your pay check. Since you didn't earn enough money to pay taxes and hadn't filed for an exemption on your W-4 form, you must file an income-tax return in order to get back the $324.17 withheld. You will need the W-2 form that was mailed to you by your employer in January and the 1040A income-tax form. Mail the completed 1040A form and Copy B of your W-2 form to the Internal Revenue Service no later than April 15.

Here's how you file for your refund, using the 1040A form and the instruction booklet that comes with it. I am assuming you are not married. The following steps correspond with the numbers in the left margin of the sample 1040A form:
1. Fill in your name, address, Social Security number, and occupation.
2. Do not check the Presidential-Election-Campaign-Fund box because you are not paying taxes.

Department of the Treasury—Internal Revenue Service
U.S. Individual Income Tax Return 19**79**

Use IRS label. Otherwise, please print or type.	Your first name and initial (if joint return, also give spouse's name and initial) MARY P	Last name WHITE	Your social security number 631 18 7284
	Present home address (Number and street, including apartment number, or rural route) 51 Hope Ln.		Spouse's social security no.
	City, town or post office, State and ZIP code ANY Town, USA 12345	Your occupation ▶ Clerk, Student Spouse's occupation ▶	

Presidential Election Campaign Fund

▶ Do you want $1 to go to this fund?........... Yes ☐ No ☐

If joint return, does your spouse want $1 to go to this fund? Yes ☐ No ☐

Note: Checking "Yes" will not increase your tax or reduce your refund.

Filing Status
Check Only One Box.

1 ☒ Single
2 ☐ Married filing joint return (even if only one had income)
3 ☐ Married filing separate return. Enter spouse's social security number above and full name here ▶
4 ☐ Head of household. (See page 8 of Instructions.) If qualifying person is your unmarried child, enter child's name ▶

For Privacy Act Notice, see page 14 of Instructions

Exemptions
Always check the box labeled Yourself. Check other boxes if they apply.

5a ☒ Yourself	65 or over ☐	Blind ☐	Enter number of boxes checked on 5a and b ▶	1
b ☐ Spouse	65 or over ☐	Blind ☐		

c First names of your dependent children who lived with you ▶ — Enter number of children listed ▶

d Other dependents: (1) Name	(2) Relationship	(3) Number of months lived in your home.	(4) Did dependent have income of $1,000 or more?	(5) Did you provide more than one-half of dependent's support?

Enter number of other dependents ▶

6 Total number of exemptions claimed .... Add numbers entered in boxes above ▶

7 Wages, salaries, tips, etc. (Attach Forms W-2. If you do not have a W-2, see page 10 of Instructions)	**7**	2380	00
8 Interest income (See pages 4 and 10 of Instructions)	**8**		
9a Dividends _____ (See pages 4 and 10 of Instructions) 9b Exclusion _____ Subtract line 9b from 9a	**9c**		
10a Unemployment compensation. Total amount received _____			
b Taxable part, if any, from worksheet on page 11 of Instructions	**10b**		
11 Adjusted gross income (add lines 7, 8, 9c, and 10b). If under $10,000, see page 2 of Instructions on "Earned Income Credit."	**11**	2380	00
12a Credit for contributions to candidates for public office. (See page 11 of Instructions) 12a			
IF YOU WANT IRS TO FIGURE YOUR TAX, PLEASE STOP HERE AND SIGN BELOW.			
b Total Federal income tax withheld (If line 7 is more than $22,900, see page 12 of Instructions) 12b 324 17			
c Earned income credit (from page 2 of Instructions) 12c			
13 Total (add lines 12a, b, and c)	**13**	324	17
14a Tax on the amount on line 11. (See Instructions for line 14a on page 12; then find your tax in the Tax Tables on pages 15–26.) 14a			
b Advance earned income credit payments received (from Form W-2) 14b			
15 Total (add lines 14a and 14b)	**15**	0	
16 If line 13 is larger than line 15, enter amount to be **REFUNDED TO YOU** ...... ▶	**16**	324	17
17 If line 15 is larger than line 13, enter **BALANCE DUE.** Attach check or money order for full amount payable to "Internal Revenue Service." Write your social security number on check or money order. ▶	**17**		

Under penalties of perjury, I declare that I have examined this return, including accompanying schedules and statements, and to the best of my knowledge and belief it is true, correct, and complete. Declaration of preparer (other than taxpayer) is based on all information of which preparer has any knowledge.

Your signature *Mary P. White* Date *Feb 18, 1980*

Spouse's signature (if filing jointly, BOTH must sign even if only one had income)

Paid Preparer's Information	Preparer's signature and date ▶	Check if self-employed ▶ ☐	Preparer's social security no.
	Firm's name (or yours, if self-employed) and address ▶	E.I. No. ▶ ZIP code ▶	

☆ U.S. Government Printing Office: 1979—0-283-317   23-0918756

Form **1040A** (1979)

Filing for a refund if you've earned less than the minimum taxable income

3. Check "single" under filing status.
4. Under exemptions, list yourself in the box on line 5a and write 1 (one) on the right. A single person without dependents may claim only one exemption.
5. On line 7, enter your total wages, as shown in blank 10 of your W-2 form. In this sample, it is $2,380.00.
6. Since you have no other income, repeat that number on line 11.
7. On line 12b, write in the amount of the federal income tax withheld from your salary, shown in Box 9 of your W-2 form ($324.17). Since lines 12a and 12c don't apply to you, repeat this amount on line 13.
8. You owe no taxes, so you enter 0 on line 15.
9. Since the amount on line 13 is $324.17 and the tax owed (line 15) is zero, you have overpaid your taxes by $324.17. Enter this amount on line 16.
10. Sign and date your return, attach Copy B of your W-2 form, and mail it to the Internal Revenue Service. Note that the W-2 form is attached (stapled, taped, or clipped) at the left-hand margin halfway down the form.
11. Your refund check for $324.17 should come in the mail in four to six weeks. Happy spending!

Filing for a Refund When You've Earned More Than the Minimum Taxable Income

The only difference in filing when you've earned more than the minimum is that you will have to determine how much tax is due. Note lines 13, 15, and 16 of the 1040A form.

Using Tax Table A, shown on page 48, determine the tax to be entered on lines 14a and 15. If, for example, your adjusted gross income is $3,780, your tax would be $67.00. This figure is based on a single filing status with an income of more than $3,750.00 but less than $3,800.00. Since the figure on line 13 ($94.80) is larger than $67.00, enter your overpayment of $27.80 on line 16.

Filing When You Owe More Taxes Than Have Been Withheld

If the figure on line 13 of your 1040A form is smaller than the one on line 15, you enter the difference on line 17. This means you owe additional taxes and must mail a check or money order

Left form:

ot have a W-2, see page 10 of	7	37 80
	8	
ion Subtract line 9b from 9a	9c	
ons	10a	
der $10,000, see page 2 of in-	11	37 80
	12a	
P HERE AND SIGN BELOW.	12b	94 80
	12c	
	13	94 80
	14a	67 00
	14b	
DED TO YOU ▶	15	67 00
check or money order for full amount nber on check or money order ▶	16	27 80
	17	

Right form:

ot have a W-2, see page 10 of	7	4165 00
	8	
ion Subtract line 9b from 9a	9c	
ons	10a	
der $10,000, see page 2 of in-	11	4165 00
	12a	
P HERE AND SIGN BELOW.	12b	115 00
	12c	
	13	115 00
	14a	123 00
	14b	
DED TO YOU ▶	15	123 00
check or money order for full amount nber on check or money order ▶	16	
	17	8 00

Line 16 of the 1040A shows the amount of your refund. If you owe more taxes than have been withheld, the amount you must pay is shown on line 17.

for that amount to the Internal Revenue Service along with your W-2 and 1040A forms.

FOOD SHOPPING

Stretching your food dollar as far as it will go is a time-honored budgeting trick. Here are some tips that will help.

- Try to shop alone.
- Don't shop when you are hungry.
- Check advertised specials in the paper and plan your menu around them.
- Make a list at home and stick to it (no impulse buying).
- Pay for your groceries with cash. If you use a check, you're apt to buy on impulse.
- The coupons you get in the mail or cut from your newspaper or magazine can save quite a bit on your grocery bills, but don't let them be an excuse for buying something you don't need.

1979 Tax Table A

Single (Filing Status Box 1)

(For single persons with income of $20,000 or less on Form 1040A, line 11, who claim 3 or fewer exemptions)

To find your tax: Read down the income column until you find your income as shown on Form 1040A, line 11. Read across to the column headed by the total number of exemptions claimed on

Form 1040A, line 6. The amount shown where the two lines meet is your tax. Enter on Form 1040A, line 14a.

The $2,300 zero bracket amount and your deduction for exemptions have been taken into account in figuring the tax shown in this table. Do not take a separate deduction for them.

Caution: If you can be claimed as a dependent on your parent's return AND you have unearned income (interest, dividends, etc.) of $1,000 or more AND your earned income is less than $2,300, you must use Form 1040.

If Form 1040A, line 11, is—		And the total number of exemptions claimed on line 6 is—			If Form 1040A, line 11, is—		And the total number of exemptions claimed on line 6 is—			If Form 1040A, line 11, is—		And the total number of exemptions claimed on line 6 is-		
Over	But not over	1	2	3	Over	But not over	1	2	3	Over	But not over	1	2	3
		Your tax is—					Your tax is—					Your tax is—		
If $3,300 or less your tax is 0					5,900	5,950	409	238	88	8,500	8,550	887	697	517
3,300	3,350	4	0	0	5,950	6,000	418	246	95	8,550	8,600	896	706	526
3,350	3,400	11	0	0	6,000	6,050	427	254	102	8,600	8,650	906	716	535
3,400	3,450	18	0	0	6,050	6,100	436	262	109	8,650	8,700	915	725	544
3,450	3,500	25	0	0										
					6,100	6,150	445	270	116	8,700	8,750	925	735	553
3,500	3,550	32	0	0	6,150	6,200	454	278	123	8,750	8,800	934	744	562
3,550	3,600	39	0	0	6,200	6,250	463	286	130	8,800	8,850	944	754	571
3,600	3,650	46	0	0	6,250	6,300	472	294	137	8,850	8,900	953	763	580
3,650	3,700	53	0	0										
					6,300	6,350	481	302	144	8,900	8,950	963	773	589
3,700	3,750	60	0	0	6,350	6,400	490	310	151	8,950	9,000	972	782	598
★ 3,750	3,800	67	0	0	6,400	6,450	499	319	158	9,000	9,050	982	792	607
3,800	3,850	74	0	0	6,450	6,500	508	328	166	9,050	9,100	991	801	616
3,850	3,900	81	0	0										
					6,500	6,550	517	337	174	9,100	9,150	1,001	811	625
3,900	3,950	88	0	0	6,550	6,600	526	346	182	9,150	9,200	1,010	820	634
3,950	4,000	95	0	0	6,600	6,650	535	355	190	9,200	9,250	1,020	830	643
4,000	4,050	102	0	0	6,650	6,700	544	364	198	9,250	9,300	1,029	839	652
4,050	4,100	109	0	0										
					6,700	6,750	553	373	206	9,300	9,350	1,039	849	661
4,100	4,150	116	0	0	6,750	6,800	562	382	214	9,350	9,400	1,048	858	670
★ 4,150	4,200	123	0	0	6,800	6,850	571	391	222	9,400	9,450	1,058	868	679
4,200	4,250	130	0	0	6,850	6,900	580	400	230	9,450	9,500	1,067	877	688
4,250	4,300	137	0	0										
					6,900	6,950	589	409	238	9,500	9,550	1,077	887	697
4,300	4,350	144	4	0	6,950	7,000	598	418	246	9,550	9,600	1,088	896	706
4,350	4,400	151	11	0	7,000	7,050	607	427	254	9,600	9,650	1,098	906	716
4,400	4,450	158	18	0	7,050	7,100	616	436	262	9,650	9,700	1,109	915	725
4,450	4,500	166	25	0										
					7,100	7,150	625	445	270	9,700	9,750	1,119	925	735
4,500	4,550	174	32	0	7,150	7,200	634	454	278	9,750	9,800	1,130	934	744
4,550	4,600	182	39	0	7,200	7,250	643	463	286	9,800	9,850	1,140	944	754
4,600	4,650	190	46	0	7,250	7,300	652	472	294	9,850	9,900	1,151	953	763
4,650	4,700	198	53	0										
					7,300	7,350	661	481	302	9,900	9,950	1,161	963	773
4,700	4,750	206	60	0	7,350	7,400	670	490	310	9,950	10,000	1,172	972	782
4,750	4,800	214	67	0	7,400	7,450	679	499	319	10,000	10,050	1,182	982	792
4,800	4,850	222	74	0	7,450	7,500	688	508	328	10,050	10,100	1,193	991	801
4,850	4,900	230	81	0										
					7,500	7,550	697	517	337	10,100	10,150	1,203	1,001	811
4,900	4,950	238	88	0	7,550	7,600	706	526	346	10,150	10,200	1,214	1,010	820
4,950	5,000	246	95	0	7,600	7,650	716	535	355	10,200	10,250	1,224	1,020	830
5,000	5,050	254	102	0	7,650	7,700	725	544	364	10,250	10,300	1,235	1,029	839
5,050	5,100	262	109	0										
					7,700	7,750	735	553	373	10,300	10,350	1,245	1,039	849
5,100	5,150	270	116	0	7,750	7,800	744	562	382	10,350	10,400	1,256	1,048	858
5,150	5,200	278	123	0	7,800	7,850	754	571	391	10,400	10,450	1,266	1,058	868
5,200	5,250	286	130	0	7,850	7,900	763	580	400	10,450	10,500	1,277	1,067	877
5,250	5,300	294	137	0										
					7,900	7,950	773	589	409	10,500	10,550	1,287	1,077	887
5,300	5,350	302	144	4	7,950	8,000	782	598	418	10,550	10,600	1,298	1,088	896
5,350	5,400	310	151	11	8,000	8,050	792	607	427	10,600	10,650	1,308	1,098	906
5,400	5,450	319	158	18	8,050	8,100	801	616	436	10,650	10,700	1,319	1,109	915
5,450	5,500	328	166	25										
					8,100	8,150	811	625	445	10,700	10,750	1,329	1,119	925
5,500	5,550	337	174	32	8,150	8,200	820	634	454	10,750	10,800	1,340	1,130	934
5,550	5,600	346	182	39	8,200	8,250	830	643	463	10,800	10,850	1,350	1,140	944
5,600	5,650	355	190	46	8,250	8,300	839	652	472	10,850	10,900	1,361	1,151	953
5,650	5,700	364	198	53										
					8,300	8,350	849	661	481	10,900	10,950	1,371	1,161	963
5,700	5,750	373	206	60	8,350	8,400	858	670	490	10,950	11,000	1,382	1,172	972
5,750	5,800	382	214	67	8,400	8,450	868	679	499	11,000	11,050	1,392	1,182	982
5,800	5,850	391	222	74	8,450	8,500	877	688	508	11,050	11,100	1,403	1,193	991
5,850	5,900	400	230	81										
Continued next column					Continued next column					Continued on next page				

Page 1 of Tax Table A

- Try to shop for canned goods, paper products, and vegetables at co-op stores, no-frill stores, or warehouse markets. Prices will be lower because of the low overhead.

You should know certain things about canned goods.

- They don't last forever. A year is the normal shelf life.
- Stores often sell dented canned goods at a discount. Take advantage of these discounts, but use the cans quickly. *Don't* buy any can that has swollen or bulging ends or seams. Such cans may contain poisoned food.
- Buy "house" or "generic" brands. The labels of generic foods do not carry brand names, but list only the contents of the can. Because they are not advertised, generic canned goods are cheaper.
- The law requires that canned and packaged foods carry a list of their ingredients in the order of the amounts contained. The product contains the largest percentage of the first item listed, and so on. The list of ingredients can be a clue to value. Check, for example, whether a can of chili lists meat first or beans first.
- Nutritional information is also available on the labels of canned goods, so be sure to check—especially if you are buying an item for the first time.

When buying dairy products (milk, cheese) or bakery goods (breads, potato chips), check the dates stamped on them. By law, the store may not sell these goods after the dates marked on the packages. All dairy products can be used for about one week after the date marked if they are properly stored.

The United States Department of Agriculture (USDA) grades beef, lamb, and veal produced in the United States with one of five labels:

- USDA Prime: This is the most tender, juicy, and expensive. The fat content is high.
- USDA Choice: It is juicy, flavorful, and popular. The fat content is high, but not as high as in Prime.
- USDA Good: Fairly tender, this grade is leaner than higher grades. It can be a good buy.

- USDA Standard: Less flavorful and tender, it has a higher proportion of lean meat to fat.
- USDA Commercial: It has a lot of marbling with fat, but it comes from older animals and must be cooked a long time with moist heat, like pot roast, for instance.

Most of the meat in supermarkets is Choice; however, much of it is Good or Standard. The lower grades have a lower fat content, and therefore are both more nutritious and cheaper.

RAIN CHECKS

If you go to a store to buy something that has been advertised, but the store has run out of the item, ask for a "rain check." This will allow you to return when the item is in stock and buy it at the advertised price.

BRAND-NAME RATINGS

You've decided to buy a new toaster—or automobile, stereo, ski jacket, electric drill, or practically anything that you expect to pay quite a bit for. How do you find out which brand will best suit your needs?

A number of organizations publish magazines or books for consumers. *Shopper's Guide,* published by the United States Department of Agriculture and *Consumer's Report,* published by Consumer's Union, are available at your local library.

Consumer organizations buy a wide range of products of various brands and subject them to tests. Then they publish the test results along with a brand-name preference for each product.

BARGAINING

There are surprisingly few places where a little bargaining does not result in an occasional price reduction. We all understand that bargaining is part of the game at a swap meet, a used-car lot (or a new one, for that matter), or in a private sales transaction. Here are four additional bargaining opportunities that may not have crossed your mind:

- Ask a retailer for a reduction when you buy with cash or a check instead of a credit card.
- At large chains, such as Sears, Penney's, or Montgomery

Ward, ask sales clerks when the next sale is planned for the item you want. They usually know.
• Look for slightly damaged goods in any store, then ask the floor or department manager for a discount.
• *Always* bargain in second-hand stores, in private transactions, when buying a car, with stores that cater to tourists, and with real-estate people.

REPAIRS

A habit we've fallen into in this affluent country is to throw away items, large or small, when they become damaged or stop working. Most appliances and pieces of furniture, however, can be repaired, and for much less than it would cost to replace them. Every town has shops that provide repair services. In general they are both honest and skillful. A few precautions, however, can help you avoid paying more than you're willing to spend for repairs.

Whenever you take anything to a repair shop, be sure to ask what the repairs will cost. You will usually receive either a firm price or an estimate. If you receive an estimate or are told that an estimate can't be given until the item is torn down and examined, leave your telephone number and instructions to be called and given a firm price before the item is actually repaired. This practice will protect you from being stuck with excessive repair bills.

HEATING-BILL SAVER (SOMETIMES)

In some areas of the country you can save money by burning wood instead of oil. The warmth and cheer of a fire in your fireplace—if you're lucky enough to have one—is increased by the knowledge that you are saving both fossil fuels and money. Wood-burning stoves are also regaining popularity. If you cut your own wood, the saving can be substantial. Many people who can't cut their own wood can buy it, either by the cord or the half cord. Remember how much wood is in a cord so you won't be cheated.

A cord of wood is a stack of 4-foot-long pieces of wood piled 4 feet high and 8 feet across. A face cord is wood cut to fireplace length (18 to 24 inches) piled 4 feet high and 8 feet across. Face cords contain only about half as much wood as standard cords.

Look for dry hardwood for a long-lasting fire. Dry wood will have some cracks in the cut edge.

TIPPING

There are no hard-and-fast rules of tipping, but the following is a guide:

- Waitress or waiter: 15% of bill, unless you get super service; then it should be 20%
- Wine steward: 10% of the cost of the wine
- Bartender: 15% of the cost of the drink
- Sky cap: 35¢ per bag
- Bellman: 50¢ to $1 per bag
- Chambermaid: $1 per night
- Hairdresser: 20% of bill. Where services are split, 15% to hairdresser, 5% to shampoo girl.
- Barber: 50¢ per haircut. 20% of bill if you have a hair stylist do it
- Cab driver: 15% to 20% of fare
- Ladies' or men's room attendant: 50¢ if he or she helps you in some way. No tip for just using the facilities
- Doorman: 25¢ if he hails a cab for you

METRIC MEASUREMENTS

As the United States moves closer to adopting metric measurements, you'll find more and more metric notations on products. The metric system is based on units of 10—10, 100, 1000, and so on. Prefixes are used to change the value of the measurement:

deci = $^1/_{10}$	*deca* = 10 times
centi = $^1/_{100}$	*hecto* = 100 times
milli = $^1/_{1000}$	*kilo* = 1000 times

For example:

1 *deci*meter = $^1/_{10}$ meter	1 *deca*meter = 10 meters
1 *centi*meter = $^1/_{100}$ meter	1 *hecto*meter = 100 meters
1 *milli*meter = $^1/_{1000}$ meter	1 *kilo*meter = 1000 meters

In general, a kilogram is 2.2 pounds, a liter is a tiny bit more than a quart, a meter is a little longer than a yard, and a kilometer is a little over a half-mile. Here are some useful conversions:

VOLUME
1 pint = .473 liter
1 quart = .946 liter
1 gallon = 3.785 liters
1 liter = 1.057 quarts
1 imperial gallon = 1.057 U.S. gallons

LENGTH
1 inch = 2.54 centimeters
1 foot = 30.48 centimeters
1 yard = .9144 meter
1 mile = 1.6093 kilometers
1 centimeter = .393 inches
1 meter = 39.37 inches
1 kilometer = .6214 miles

WEIGHT
1 ounce = 28.35 grams
1 pound = .4536 kilograms
1 gram = .03527 ounce
1 kilogram = 2.2046 pounds

TEMPERATURE	Fahrenheit (U.S.)	Centigrade or Celsius (Metric)
Freezing	32°F.	0°C.
Comfort zone	70°F.	21°C.
Body temperature	98.6°F.	37°C.
Boiling point	212°F.	100°C.

STOCKS AND BONDS

We have all heard about people who have earned fortunes in the stock market—and about others who have gone broke. I won't advise you to invest, nor will I advise you against it. What I will do is explain it.

The stock market, like any other market, is a place where merchandise is bought and sold. The merchandise is stocks and bonds. The people behind the counters are brokerage house employees who accept orders to buy or sell at the going price that day—called "at market."

What is a stock? What is a bond? A *stock* is a share in the ownership of a company, entitling the buyer to a proportionate share in the profits. A *bond* is a loan made to the government or a business firm for a limited period of time at a fixed annual rate of interest.

Your daily newspaper lists all the stocks traded on the New York Stock Exchange and the American Stock Exchange, as well as a few that are of interest in your locality, which are traded on the "Over-the-Counter" market.

Let's look at the fine print that makes up the stock-market listings:

	P.E.	Sales (hds.)	High	Low	Close	Chg.
EZY–3.60	11	975	53 7/8	53 1/4	53 5/8	+ 1/4

"EZY" is the abbreviation of the name of the company.

The "3.60" is $3.60, the yearly stock dividend, which is paid quarterly.

"P.E." means price-earnings ratio, the ratio between the market price of the stock and the company's earnings. In this example the investor is paying $11 for each $1 of company earnings. The P.E. reflects the confidence that those who invested on that day had in the company's future.

The "975" in hundreds (hds.) means that 97,500 shares were bought and sold at the market that day.

High 53 7/8 means that $53.875 was the highest price of the day.

Low 53 1/4 means that $53.25 was the lowest price of the day.

Close 53 5/8 means that $53.625 was the price of the last transaction of the day.

Chg. + 1/4 means that there was a change (*Chg.*) of + 1/4, or 1/4 of a point. A point is $1.00. Therefore, there was an increase of 25¢ for the day.

The list for the American Stock Exchange reads the same way.

Over-the-Counter transactions read:

Name of Stock	Bid	Asked
Ski Slopes	3 1/2	4 1/8

Bid is the highest price the buyer is offering to pay.

Asked is the lowest price the seller will accept.

When someone asks, "How's the Dow doing today?" and someone else answers, "It's up four points," that means that the average price for the thirty "industrials" (stock of industrial companies) making up the Dow Jones Average is up four points, meaning up $4.00.

There are several current stock market averages, but the Dow, though not necessarily the most accurate, is the most often quoted.

If you're interested in the stock market, you might try *pretending* to purchase two or three issues. Write down what you pretend to buy, the quantity, and the price. Then watch the stock listings in the newspaper for a few months to get an idea of how much money you would have gained or lost. Try it. It's fun!

DIAMONDS, GOLD, AND SILVER

Diamonds, gold, and silver are always valuable as well as beautiful. You may not be able to afford to invest in any of them right now, but they are worth considering if you *can* afford to invest.

For about twenty dollars you can get certification from the Gemological Institute of America (GIA) on the genuineness of any diamond over one carat in weight. Your jeweler will have the necessary forms to send to the GIA.

Any reputable jeweler can give you printed information on the subject. *Diamonds,* a booklet published by the American Gem Society, will help you choose a diamond.

If you would like to buy diamond jewelry right now but find that you can't, there is an alternative. The art of making synthetic diamonds has progressed so much that it's difficult for anyone but an expert to distinguish the genuine from the imitation. Consumer organizations have taken real diamonds and imitations to various retail jewelers. In one survey, four out of eight failed to tell them apart. If you're planning to get married and your budget doesn't include the cost of a diamond, you may want to buy a cheaper, synthetic stone now and a real one later, perhaps for a wedding anniversary.

Gold is the most precious of metals. Its quality is measured in carats (K)—24K is pure gold, too soft to make jewelry from. The finest gold used in jewelry is 22K. The most commonly used are 10K, 14K, and 18K. A 12K gold item is only 50 percent gold.

Many pieces of gold jewelry are "plated," which means they have a surface coating of gold over another metal. When an item is marked "12K RGP," the base metal has been "rolled gold plated" with gold of 12K purity. "Gold filled" means that the base metal has been electroplated with a thin film of gold.

Silver is one of the most beautiful and versatile of metals. It's also very valuable, and you should be sure you know what you're buying. The word "sterling" will be imprinted on the back of any object that's at least 92 ½ percent pure silver. Any item that's silver plated may not legally have the word "sterling" imprinted on it. Beware of "stirling," "sperling," or other deliberate "look-alikes." They are guarantees of shoddy merchandise.

The Commerce Department's Trademark Office recently ruled that imported and American-made gold and silver products must have a karat-quality and trademark imprinted on them. The trademark guarantees the precious-metal content of the product. If you're buying a piece of gold or silver, ask to see the karat mark and the registered trademark of the company that guarantees the gold or silver content.

5 | Banking

Banks are reputedly managed by sedate people who routinely stuff money into various accounts and balance them to the very penny every evening before they go home. No so! Not always, anyway.

We'll never forget the time my husband made a small deposit in his savings account that panicked our bank for almost three weeks. Quite routinely, and by mistake, someone punched his account number into the computer instead of the amount of his deposit, and his savings account immediately swelled by $2,853,471! We found out about it when the operations officer called us and told us that the bank was reducing our savings account by that amount. The bank officer sounded tired, and I guess she was, because she said that bank personnel had spent the last twenty days and evenings trying to find their mistake.

You'll find, however, that the mistakes a bank may make are outweighed by the safety, convenience, and service they offer.

How much money should you have before you get acquainted with your local bank? There's no hard and fast rule, but in general you should begin banking as soon as you have bills to pay or money to save. Certainly when you've landed that first job, you'll want the convenience of paying bills by check, and a place to save for a rainy day.

Most people choose a bank because it is near their home or job. Before you settle on a bank simply because of its location, check the cost of the services you want. A bank or savings and loan association is a business that *needs customers* in order to make a profit, and it wants *you*. Different banks charge different amounts for checking services and pay different interest rates on savings, so be a good shopper. Many services that each provides are identical, while others have important differences. After determining your banking needs, phone or visit small, medium-sized, and large banks and compare their services and costs. Remember, too, that these costs may vary in different branches of the same bank. Smaller banks usually offer more extra services in order to compete with larger banks.

There is really nothing complicated about doing business with a bank, savings and loan association, or credit union. However, there are some important things to know and look for, and this chapter will be your guide.

BANKING TERMS

As you read through this chapter you will come across many terms that are used by banks. Although you are probably familiar with most of them, this list of definitions will be helpful.

ACCOUNT: a record of the amount of money on deposit in a bank that can be withdrawn by the depositor.

BALANCE: the total amount of money in an account at any given time.

CHECK: a written order to a bank for money payable to the person named on the check.

CHECKING ACCOUNT: a bank account against which the depositor can write checks any time, without a passbook.

COMPOUND INTEREST: money paid by the bank on money you have deposited and on the interest that has already accumulated.

CREDIT: when you have proved that you pay your debts on time, you have established *credit*. Your bank will then be willing to lend you money or to issue you a *credit card*.

CREDITED: refers to any amount that's *added to* your account.

DEBITED: refers to any amount that's *subtracted from* your account.

DEPOSIT: money put into your bank account, or *credited* to your account.

ENDORSE: to sign your name on the back of a check at the time you cash it in order to receive the money.

FDIC (Federal Deposit Insurance Corporation): protects your money in commercial banks.

FSLIC (Federal Savings and Loan Insurance Corporation): protects your money in savings and loan associations.

INTEREST: money paid to you by the bank on money you have *deposited,* or money paid by you to the bank on money you have *borrowed.*

LOAN: money lent to you by a bank in return for your written promise to repay, on a regular schedule, both the money and *interest* on the money.

MORTGAGE: a document you sign when you borrow money from a bank to buy a house or a car, which states that the bank owns a share of the house or car until the debt is paid.

NCUA (National Credit Union Administration): protects your money in credit unions.

PASSBOOK: a small book in which you or the bank teller records debits and credits to your savings account.

SAVINGS ACCOUNT: a bank account designed to help you save money. The bank pays interest on the amounts you deposit. Until recently checks could not be written on a savings account.

S. & L.: abbreviation for savings and loan banks.

TIME DEPOSIT: a type of savings account from which money cannot be withdrawn for a certain length of time (six months to years, depending on your agreement with the bank); also called *certificate of deposit.*

WITHDRAWAL: money you take out of your savings account.

TYPES OF BANKS

We've had a houseful of banks since Santa Claus slid a piggy bank down the laundry chute (we didn't have a chimney) on our first son's first Christmas. We've had slot-machine banks, reach-out-and-grab-the-coin banks, combination-lock-safe banks, automatic-add-and-show-the-total banks, pry-proof banks, and eighty-three other kinds I can't even remember. I don't think we ever had more than five dollars in any one of them before it was "accidentally" smashed with a sledge hammer. I recommend none of these for you. Let's look at those that can help you.

WARNING: Make sure that the bank you invest in displays one of these signs:

FDIC

FSLIC

NCUA

These signs show that the banks are insured by the United States government. If the bank should fail, the government will pay back your money up to $40,000 per person. Many people have lost their entire savings by placing their money in banks that do not have insurance.

- Commercial full-service bank: Full-service banks provide virtually all banking services, including checking accounts, savings accounts, loans, bank cards (credit cards), safety-deposit boxes, financial counseling, and automatic payment of your bills. The list goes on and on. There are variations at different banks, but they are basically the same. *If you decide to start an account at a full-service bank, make sure it displays this sign:*

MEMBER FDIC

- Savings and loan association: The S. & L. is a place to save and borrow money. It does *not* offer checking accounts but usually provides a higher interest rate on your savings. *Be sure the S. & L. you plan to use displays this sign:*

FSLIC

- Credit union: A nonprofit association made up of people with a common bond (such as employees of the same company or members of a union), a credit union *cannot offer you a checking account.* The main reason for belonging to a credit union is that you can borrow money easily. It also offers good interest rates on savings accounts. *Be sure any credit union you are interested in displays this sign:*

MEMBER NCUA

SAVINGS ACCOUNTS

The two main reasons for having a savings account are that a bank is a safe place for your money, and you collect interest for letting the bank use your money. It's a good idea to open a savings account, even with a minimum of $5.00. It is a great credit reference if you need one.

Important Things to Look For

- The savings account must be federally insured.
- Interest should be computed *from the day you deposit until the day you withdraw.*
- Interest should be *compounded and credited daily.* This means that every day a small interest is added to your account so that you are really earning interest on interest. There are more than fifty-four ways to compute interest. Interest computed and credited daily will give you the most for your money.
- The bank should offer the highest interest, but don't forget that equally important is how often the interest is compounded and credited. Savings and loans and credit unions usually offer the highest interest on savings accounts.
- There is a limit of free withdrawals on some accounts, usually three withdrawals in three months. If you withdraw four times in three months, you will be charged a fee for each withdrawal. Check with your bank. Each one is different.
- Some savings accounts have "grace days," which allow you to deposit funds any time during the first ten days of a new interest-payment period, and you receive interest for the entire period.
- By opening a savings account you may receive some of the following: safety-deposit box, money orders, travelers checks, notary services, or automatic payment of monthly bills. You usually need a fairly high minimum balance to rate these free services, but *ask.*

Warnings About Savings

Do not save in savings accounts that:

- Pay interest on the *lowest balance* in your account for an entire interest period.
- Require that you have a *minimum balance* before you earn interest.

Types of Savings Accounts

There are two main types of savings accounts: regular savings and time-deposit accounts.

- Regular savings account is an account from which you can withdraw your money any time, but the interest paid is the lowest the bank offers.
- A time deposit is an account requiring that you leave your money for a certain length of time (from ninety days up to ten years), but you receive a higher interest rate. A minimum of $1,000 to $5,000 is usually required to open a time deposit. If you don't leave your money for the period agreed upon, your interest will usually be recalculated at the regular savings-account rate and you will lose interest earned for a ninety-day period before you withdraw your money. You should use time-deposit only if you are certain you will be able to leave the money for the time agreed upon. The penalty for withdrawing earlier is very heavy.

Opening a Savings Account

Once you have decided on the bank or savings and loan association you will use, the procedure for setting up a savings account is quite simple.

A bank employee will help you fill out the necessary papers. You then deposit your money, and the bank will issue a passbook and a receipt for the total amount of the money deposited. The passbook is a record of your deposits and withdrawals as well as a record of your balance and the interest paid on that balance. You can deposit and withdraw from your account *without* your passbook in some banks. For this reason, it is *very important* that you *keep all deposit receipts* issued by your bank. Your passbook is not an official receipt. Banks make mistakes, and without your bank-issued receipt your account will be almost impossible to correct.

Savings Deposits

Your first deposit will be taken care of by the bank teller. However, from then on you will have to fill out a deposit slip for each new deposit. The deposit slips are usually colored and are found on the tables in the bank.

A deposit slip includes a blank for a cash deposit and several blanks for checks, since each check must be listed separately. Fill in the blanks, add up your figures, then write in the total amount of your deposit in the blank provided for that purpose at the bottom. Take the filled-out deposit slip to the teller, and he or she will enter the amount in your passbook. In some banks the teller will also give you a deposit receipt. Be sure to save the deposit receipts in case the bank makes an error. Deposit slips are not exactly alike in all banks, but the procedure for filling them in is essentially the same.

About every three months some banks send you a savings statement in the mail. You will then be able to check your deposit receipts against the bank's official records. If you want to know the amount of your savings balance before your statement arrives, call or go into the bank and a clerk will give it to you.

Again, remember that each bank has its own procedure. Some savings banks do not send out statements. They expect you to keep a record of your transactions in your passbook. Also, many banks will not give you balance information over the telephone.

Savings Withdrawals

When you wish to take some of your money out of a savings account, fill out a savings-withdrawal slip. These are also found on the tables in the banks. Some banks issue savings deposit and withdrawal slips with your savings-account number printed on them when you open your account. In any case you should be familiar with the slips and know how to fill them out. Take the filled out withdrawal slip and your passbook to the bank teller to receive your money.

CHECKING ACCOUNTS

Checks have been a form of exchange in the United States since Revolutionary times. In those days they were a crude form of what we have today. There have been cases of checks (which are really nothing more than written orders to your bank requesting it to pay money) having been scrawled on animal skins, birch bark, paper sacks, and even on a fresh egg!

Today's checks are made by highly sophisticated computer systems that respond to the numbers in the left-hand corner of the magnetic ink character recognition (MICR) code. Those numbers represent the city where the bank account is located, the bank's name, the branch, and the account number. Computer systems enable modern banks to keep up with the tremendous amount of paperwork they must deal with.

Checking allows you to keep money in a safe place where you can get it easily, and most important, it gives you a record of your payments.

The Cost of Checking

There are usually expenses involved in having a checking account. The cost of an account varies according to the number of checks you write monthly, and the type of account you have. By estimating your banking needs before deciding on the type of account to open, you can cut down on these costs. Try to figure out about how many checks you will write in a month and the approximate minimum balance you must have in your account at any given time during that month.

If you think you will write about ten or fewer checks per month, you have two basic choices:

- Savings accounts: Some banks and almost all savings and loan associations let you withdraw money from your savings account whenever and as often as you like with no charge. If you need to transfer money only two or three times a month, *you might want to keep your money in a savings account, where it is receiving interest* (until recently checking accounts did not draw interest, though this is changing in many states), and make your payments with money orders. Some savings accounts offer bill-paying accounts. You list the companies and persons to whom the money should be sent, and the bank takes care of it every month. You can make changes by phoning or writing.
- Special accounts: A special checking account is designed for low check-writing needs. You pay a fee for each check you write and sometimes a monthly service charge, which varies. Checking statements are often sent quarterly (four times a year), although they may be sent monthly. Only larger banks offer this type of account.

More Than Fifteen Checks a Month

- Free checking: Some smaller banks offer completely free checking accounts, but they usually offer them to special groups such as students, civil-service employees, or senior citizens. Some larger banks have also begun to offer free checking, but only under certain conditions. Remember to ask.

- Minimum-balance accounts: This type of account is designed for someone who writes a lot of checks. You pay no charge as long as you stay above the minimum required balance during the monthly cycle. The minimum balance differs from bank to bank. Some smaller banks require only around $100. If you fall below that minimum balance, you will be charged the regular fee for checks, plus service charges.

  Remember, this type of account still isn't "free" because you do not earn interest on your account. For instance, $200 at a 5 percent interest rate would earn $10 in a year in a regular savings account.

- Package accounts: These accounts are being heavily pushed by the banks today. The reason is that the banks make a lot of money from *YOU* if you have one of these accounts. For a flat rate of $2.00 to $3.00 monthly, you receive numerous services such as unlimited check writing, automatic loans (you can write a check for more money than you have in your account, but it will be charged to your credit card), personalized checks, safety-deposit box, check-guarantee card, national bank card (Master Charge or VISA), and travelers' or cashiers' checks. Most of these are things you can easily do without. And since there is a fee, you'll find them even easier to do without.

Many of the above services are free anyway, so investigate before you commit yourself to a package account.

It Takes Money to Spend Money

More likely than not you won't be told about the extra charges you may encounter in checking. Here are three to ask about:

- Overdrafts: You must pay a fee when you write a check for a larger amount than you have in your account. Some banks charge this fee only when they cover the bad check, while others charge it whether they pay the check or not. The fees range from $2.00 to $7.50 per overdraft. Some banks give extended credit for overdrafts, but these must be paid off quickly, or you'll soon have to pay back the money with an 18-percent interest rate added on.

- Stop-payment orders: A stop-payment order cancels a check that you have written before it is cashed by the other party. This usually costs between $2.00 and $5.00, but it varies from city to city.
- Checks: Most banks provide FREE plain, colored, numbered, personalized checks, but you will almost always have to *ask for them*. You can also get scenic checks costing from $2.25 to $5.00 for 200. One question you might ask yourself is, "Do I really need big-horn sheep or flowers on my checks in order to transfer funds?"

Tips on Checking Accounts

- Look for free checking accounts.
- *Ask* for free plain, colored, numbered checks. Your address can be added for a minimum charge. (No scenic checks!)
- Check on free services provided by the bank (notary public and others).

Opening a Checking Account

After you have chosen the checking account that best suits you, the bank will help you make your first deposit. Then you will be issued a book of checks, deposit slips, and a check register to keep track of your checks. The following pages will explain how to use your checking account.

Checking Deposits

Deposit slips for your checking account are issued when you open your account and already have your account number, name, and address on them. There are also blank deposit slips at the bank that you can use should you run out or leave them at home. All deposit slips require essentially the same information:

- The date on which you are making the deposit
- Your name (sometimes preprinted)
- Your account number (sometimes preprinted)
- The amount of cash you are depositing
- The amount of each check you are depositing
- The total amount of your deposit

When you present this deposit slip with your money and checks to the teller, you will be given a deposit receipt. *Save your receipt!* You may need it in case there is a mix-up with your account.

Writing Checks (Withdrawals)

To make a withdrawal from a checking account, all you do is write a check and cash it. There are no withdrawal slips other than a check! Writing a check is very simple. About the only rules are: always use a *pen*, never sign your name to a *blank* check, and enter the amount of your checks and deposits in your check register.

Let's look at a typical check.

⑦ MARY P. WHITE   NO. ⑥ _____

DATE ① _____ 19____   91-283 / 1221

PAY TO THE ORDER OF ② _____ $ ③ _____

④ _____ DOLLARS

TEMPE REGIONAL HOME OFFICE
UNITED BANK
OF ARIZONA
64 EAST BROADWAY   TEMPE, ARIZ. 85281   ⑤

⑈1221⑈0283⑈   ⑈573510 1059⑈

A blank check

1. Write in the date.
2. Write in the name of the person to receive the check. Use real names, not nicknames.
3. Write the amount of the check, using numbers, such as $4.58, or $118.97 or $100.00.
4. Write out in *words* how many dollars your check is for. Put the *cents* in fractions. It should look like this:

   One hundred eighteen and 97/100 ——————— DOLLARS

5. Sign your name. Always sign business papers the same way. Develop a signature that you know you can write over and over again and have it look the same each time.
6. Most checks are prenumbered, but if yours are not, number them in sequence (1,2,3,4,5,6, and so on).

7. Most checks have your name and address preprinted here, but if they don't, this is where you would fill in that information, when it is required.
8. Enter amount of check or deposit in your check register.

Endorsing the Check

When you cash a check that has been made out to you by another person or company, *endorse* it on the back. To endorse a check, sign your name on the back *exactly* the same way it appears on the front. Once a check is endorsed, remember that *anyone* can cash it. It is, therefore, wise to endorse it when you cash it rather than beforehand.

How to endorse a check

If for some reason—for example, you want a friend to deposit your check at your bank—you do decide to endorse your check before cashing it, you can endorse your check this way:

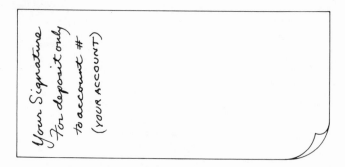

This is a safe way to endorse your check if you can't take it to the bank yourself.

There are some banks in which you might be asked to endorse someone else's check. For example, you and a friend might go to your bank to cash your checks. You endorse your check and the bank is happy to cash it because you have an account there. Your friend does not have an account at that bank and wants to cash a check written to him or her by some other person. The teller may suggest that you countersign, or endorse, your friend's check. Remember that to do so makes *you* liable in case your friend's check should bounce. If you do decide to endorse it, sign your name just below your friend's endorsement. Incidentally, many banks do not cash checks at all for people who do not have accounts there.

Balancing Your Checkbook

Balancing is a fine art.

One of the most important steps is keeping records of all the checks you write and deposits you make to your checking account. Use the check register that comes with your checks from the bank. There are many different kinds of check registers, but they all include the same information. Record all of your checking transactions on the register. Here is an example of a check register that has been kept up to date:

① CHECK NO.	② DATE	③ CHECKS ISSUED TO OR DESCRIPTION OF DEPOSIT	④ AMOUNT OF CHECK	CHECK FEE IF ANY	✓	AMOUNT OF DEPOSIT	⑤ BALANCE FORWARD 14 50
156	4/20	To Allans Shoe Shop For Socks	4 50				Bal. or Dep. 4 50
—	4/21	For DEPOSIT				27 90	Check or Dep. 10 00 / 27 90 / 37 90
157	4/26	To S.D.Simms For Doctor Bill	24 00				Check or Dep. 24 00 / 13 90
158	4/27	To Daily Blat For Newspaper	1 45				Check or Dep. 1 45 / 12 45
—	4/28	For DEPOSIT				130 40	Check or Dep. 130 40 / 142 85

Keep a record of your checks in a check register.

1. Record the check number if you are writing a check.
2. The date
3. The name of the person or firm the check is to and what it is for
4. The amount of the check, deposit, or service charges
5. Your remaining balance

Be sure to subtract $(-)$ each check you write from your balance, and add $(+)$ each deposit you make to your account.

Once a month you will receive a statement from the bank showing your checking activity for the month. Your statement is made by the bank's computers about four to five days *before* you receive it. This is one of the reasons why the statement may not show the same figures or balances that your check register shows. Your figures and the computer's may also differ because *checks you have written may not have been turned in to the bank yet; therefore that money has not yet been taken out of your account.* Many people balance their checking accounts incorrectly because they forget this.

Let's look at a sample register.

CHECK NO.	DATE	CHECKS ISSUED TO OR DESCRIPTION OF DEPOSIT	AMOUNT OF CHECK	CHECK FEE (if any)	✓	AMOUNT OF DEPOSIT	BALANCE FORWARD 74 50	
75	8/26	To Supermarket / For Groceries	16 25		✓		Check or Dep. 16 25 / Bal. 58 25	
76	9/1	To Plumber / For Sink leak	27 14		✓		Check or Dep. 27 14 / Bal. 31 11	
77	9/3	To ABC Books / For Books	10 19		✓		Check or Dep. 10 19 / Bal. 20 92	
78	9/3	To Tracy's Gift Shoppe / For Charlie's Present	4 88		✓		Check or Dep. 4 88 / Bal. 16 04	
79	9/7	To Pizza Pallazo / For 2 Pizza's	9 97		✓		Check or Dep. 9 97 / Bal. 6 07	
		To / For DEPOSIT			✓	176 50	Check or Dep. 176 50 / Bal. 182 57	
80	9/20	To Public Service Co / For Water Bill	19 02		✓		Check or Dep. 19 02 / Bal. 163 55	
—	9/21	To / For DEPOSIT			✓	37 50	Check or Dep. 37 50 / Bal. 201 05	
81	9/21	To A.L. Hofmann / For Doctor's Bill	88 17		✓		Check or Dep. 88 17 / Bal. 112 88	
82	9/22	To Supermart / For Groceries	19 50		✓		Check or Dep. 19 50 / Bal. 93 38	
83	10/2	To CHURCH / For Donation	10 00				Check or Dep. 10 00 / Bal. 83 38	
	10/4	To / For DEPOSIT				192 60	Check or Dep. 192 60 / Bal. 275 98	
	10/5	To / For DEPOSIT				21 40	Check or Dep. 21 40 / Bal. 297 38	
—	10/9	To BANK SERVICE CHARGE / For CHECKING ACCOUNT		3			Check or Dep. 3 00 / Bal. 294 38	

To balance your account, compare the bank's monthly statement with your check register.

Many banks provide space for balancing your account on their statements. If your bank does not, here are some guidelines. Let's look at the bank statement that was made out for the register we just discussed:

STATEMENT

Account Number
123-45-6789
Statement Period
3-1-80 through 4-1-80

Starting Balance: $74.50

Date	Description	Amount
8–30	Check	$ 16.25
9–3	Check	27.14
9–7	Check	10.19
9–7	Check	4.88
9–9	Deposit	176.50
9–10	Check	9.97
9–21	Deposit	37.50
9–26	Check	19.02
9–27	Check	19.50
9–30	Service Charge	3.00

Current Balance: $178.55

With this information you are ready to start balancing your checkbook. Let's do it step by step.

1. Subtract all service charges or other bank charges listed on your statement from your check register balance.

$$297.38 - 3.00 = 294.38$$

2. Review your returned checks. With your statement, you will also receive all the checks you have written for the past month *that have been returned to the bank.* Look through your check register and put a check mark ($\sqrt{}$) in the column provided if that check has been returned.

3. Add up all the deposits that are *not* shown on the statement. Go through your register and check all the deposits that *are* listed on the statement. Let's look at our examples: Add all the deposits that are not checked off in your register.

$192.60
+ 21.40
$214.00

Call this amount A. This is the total amount of deposits that the bank had not yet received at the time your statement was made.

4. Add up all the checks that are *not* checked off in your register. In this example checks numbered 81 and 83 were not returned. Add these to find the total amount of checks not returned to the bank.

$$\begin{array}{r} \$88.17 \\ +10.00 \\ \hline \$98.17 \end{array}$$

Call this amount B. This is the total amount of checking funds that are "outstanding" (not returned to the bank).

5. You are now ready to balance your checkbook with your statement. Here is a chart that makes balancing a checkbook very simple. You will probably want to write one out each month when you balance your checkbook. Let's see how easy it is.

1. Enter current balance (from bank statement).	$178.55
2. Enter total A.	+$214.00
Add total A to balance.	$392.55
3. Subtract total B.	−$ 98.17
Balanced total:	$294.38

Your balanced total should agree with your check-register balance. If it does, your checkbook is balanced and you can be assured that you will not accidentally overdraw your checking account.

If your check register does not agree with the bank statement, recheck the following:

- Make sure you have subtracted all bank service charges listed on the statement from your check register.
- Check all of your additions and subtractions.
- Review last month's statement to determine whether any differences were corrected.
- Compare all deposits and check amounts in your register with those listed on the statement.

If after all of these review procedures your checkbook still does not balance, take it in to your bank for free help in finding the trouble.

Alternatives to Checking Accounts

If you can't afford a checking account, there are other ways to protect your money and have a record of bills paid.

- Money orders: Special checks made out by the bank, post office, or any authorized money-order dealer, they are a safe way to send money through the mail and are accepted by everyone. They can be cashed only by the persons or firms you write them to, and they give you a record of your payment. You can buy a money order by giving the post office, bank teller, or authorized money-order clerk the amount of money needed up to $1,000 to pay the bill plus a service charge, which varies from state to state. They will help you write it out.

  Be sure to save the stub or carbon copy for your record of payment.
- Cashier's checks: These are purchased at any bank, much like money orders, but they are usually used when you are buying something expensive, like a car or motorcycle, and the dealer is unwilling to accept your personal check. There is a fee for these checks. Perhaps the safest way to handle a cashier's check is to have the bank make it payable to you. Then you can endorse it to the other person at the time of the transaction. This protects you if the transaction falls through and you are stuck with a cashier's check made out to someone else. (You can get your money back, but it's a hassle.)

  To endorse a cashier's check to the other party, sign the *back* of the cashier's check like this:

How to endorse a check to someone else

Other Bank Services

You should be aware of three other services offered by banks.

- Certified checks: These checks are used the same way as cashier's checks, but the bank stamps *your* own *personal* check as "certified" and reserves the money from your checking account. If you have a checking account, have your own checks certified. If not, buy a cashier's check from the bank teller.
- Travelers' checks: These are similar to money orders, in that you pay the bank when you purchase them. The difference is that *you* may cash them because they are made out in your name. They are useful when you are out of town and carrying money you can't afford to lose. Remember to keep a record of their serial numbers so that you can get your money back if the travelers' checks are lost, destroyed, or stolen.
- Safety-deposit boxes: Each of these small metal containers has its own lock and is usually kept in the bank vault. A box can be rented for a small annual fee and used to store valuables and important papers. There are two keys to each box, and both are needed to open it. The bank keeps one. You keep the other. When you store valuables in or remove them from your box, the bank will ask you to sign in, and it will verify your signature. Then the bank officer will accompany you to your box and open it for you. You can take your box to a small private room to complete your transaction. Then the bank officer will take the box and lock it with both keys.

BANKING HOT LINE

The Federal Deposit Insurance Corporation, recognizing that consumers are demanding an increasing amount of information concerning their rights with respect to banking, has opened a toll-free line to give people a chance to ask questions, give their views on banking practices, and make complaints. The number is 1-800-424-5488.

6 | Credit and Loans

My father owned a grocery store in Massachusetts during the Great Depression. Credit in those days was informal. Either a shopowner had a big heart or you went hungry. My father had a big heart, and he almost went broke feeding the neighborhood on credit. He never thought about asking for interest. In fact, he never thought about asking for payment! There was no way most people *could* pay.

We survived the depression without going bankrupt, and after Dad died in the early forties, people would show up at our home each year around Christmas, give Mom an envelope of money, and say something like, "I never got a chance to pay your husband what I owed him, but here's some on account." Mom was always surprised, because Dad hadn't kept records of what people owed him.

It's different today. Credit is easy, too easy. Creditors don't let you off the hook, though. If you use credit wisely, you'll find it to be a valuable tool. This chapter will help.

WHY DO YOU NEED CREDIT?

We live in a credit society. Most people need to finance major purchases, such as an automobile, a home, or major appliances. If you are among this majority, you should establish credit early so that it will be available when you need it.

HOW TO ESTABLISH CREDIT

To "establish credit" means to have a provable record of having repaid your loans on time. Try to obtain a gas credit card first if you have a car. Gas cards will not tempt you into impulse buying. By paying the bill over a few months, you will start a credit history. Another sure way to establish credit is to open a savings account in your bank. Then borrow at least $100 from your own savings. This is called a passbook loan. The bank will set up a repayment schedule for you. By paying these installments *on time,* you will have begun to establish a good credit history. It is helpful to arrange such a loan as soon as you can so that future credit will be available when you need it.

HOW MUCH CREDIT IS SAFE?

I've often thought that credit is like aspirin. The right amount will cure a headache, but too much will leave you sicker than you were when you started! It's necessary to establish credit, but using it unwisely always leads to financial disaster.

What is the safe dosage? How much credit should you have? An accurate rule is that you can spend 10 percent of your monthly income (after subtracting your rent payment) on installment purchases. If, for example, your monthly take-home pay is $542 and you pay $115 per month for rent, your safe limit would be figured this way:

Monthly take-home pay	$542.00
Minus rent	−115.00
	$427.00

10% of $427.00 = $42.70

You could, without overextending yourself, make monthly installment credit payments of $42.70.

CREDIT CARDS

Credit cards are excellent for scraping the frost off your car's windshield, but they make it *too* easy to impulse-buy more than you can afford.

The Cost of a Credit Card

Everyone knows that credit cards issued by stores, oil companies, and banks are free. But don't let that fool you. You pay plenty when you don't pay your entire bill each month. In fact, I suggest that until you have had several years experience in managing your own money, you do not have *any* type of bank or all-purpose credit card. Terms vary, but you can expect to pay an average of 18 percent in interest per year. That's $18 for every $100 of credit.

Here are a couple of ways of reducing that cost. If you're planning a major purchase on your credit card and intend to pay it off over a number of months, you can consider a cash advance on your credit card for the same number of months. The interest charge for a cash advance is usually about one third less than the regular credit-card interest rate.

Here's a way to use someone else's money for fifty to fifty-five days. If you make a credit card purchase just after the start of a new billing cycle, you'll receive the bill about thirty days later. You'll then have another twenty to twenty-five days to make payment before you are charged interest. You will have had the use of your purchase for almost two months before you pay a cent, and you won't be charged any interest if you pay the balance due just prior to the due date shown on your billing statement.

Before we explore other ways to buy on credit, let's examine for future use some safeguards that the law provides for credit card holders.

Legal Safeguards for Credit Card Holders

• Fair Credit Billing Act: Under this important law, you as a consumer are given rights, and the retailer has been assigned certain responsibilities:

1. If you buy an item and later find it defective and the credit card was issued by the store you bought the item from, you may legally refuse to pay for it until the item is repaired or replaced.

   Suppose you have a credit card that was *not* issued by a store. You've made a purchase of more than $50 with that credit card. You made this purchase in or outside your home state but within 100 miles of your home. In these circumstances, if the item you purchased turns out to be defective, the company that issued your credit card is required by law to help you solve your problem with the merchant. This applies to bank and all-purpose cards.

2. This law also helps solve mistakes in billing within a reasonable length of time. If you receive a bill that you believe

is in error and write to your creditor within sixty days, the law requires that the creditor respond within thirty days and that he resolve the problem within an additional ninety days.

If he doesn't correct the problem within ninety days, you may keep the first $50 of the amount in dispute, no matter whose mistake it was. You may also, if you wish, sue him for $100 plus legal fees for violating the Fair Credit Billing Act.

Truth-in-Lending Act: This is a far-reaching law, but it's worth noting two parts of it that apply to credit cards:

1. If your credit card is lost or stolen and you *immediately* notify the issuer (before charges are made with the card), you may not be made to pay for *any* charges that might be made later. Call the toll-free number on the back of your card, which you have recorded (see Chapter 4), or the store or bank that issued the card. It's important to keep a list of credit-card numbers and the phone numbers to call in case the cards are lost or stolen. Even if you *fail* to notify the issuer of a lost or stolen credit card, you may *not* be held responsible for more than $50 in charges per card.

2. Previously a company could issue a credit card whether or not you wanted it. This led to many problems because unwanted credit cards tended to get lost easily. The Truth-in-Lending Act forbids anyone to issue you a credit card unless you have asked for it. This prohibition does not apply to renewal of cards.

LOANS AND CONTRACTS

Here's the best way for most of us to buy on credit. There are a lot of do's and don't's to be aware of, but first let's define what we're talking about. We will talk about loans and contracts in the same section because each loan is governed by a contract. Even the $10 you borrow from your friend until payday represents both a loan and a contract. The $10 you get is the loan. Your promise to repay on payday is the contract.

Something to think about when considering any type of loan in periods of inflation is that dollars are worth a little less every year. The result is that it is probably cheapest to take out the longest-term loan you can get. You'll almost certainly be earning more money in the future than you're earning now, and it will be easier to make those monthly payments.

The two types of loans that are of interest to us are the installment sales contract and the personal loan.

Installment Sales Contract

The most common way to buy a TV set, furniture, or a car is on an installment sales contract. This arrangement allows you to use the item even though the seller (or the holder of the installment sales contract) has certain rights to it until the last payment is made. For example, if you can't keep up the payments, the item can be taken away—repossessed—and the seller keeps all the money you have paid. The seller can resell the item, but if he doesn't get enough money to cover what you still owe on the loan, you must repay that amount. For example, if you bought a car for $900 and paid the seller $400 in installment payments before you lost your job and couldn't keep up the payments, the seller would take your car back. Suppose he resells it for $300. You still owe $200! If he sells the car for $600, he owes you $100! This hardly ever happens, though.

Installment Loan Contracts (Personal Loans)

When you need to borrow money for your own use, to pay your debts, for instance, you will take out a personal loan. The lender will want something as security, perhaps your car or motorcycle, before he will give you the money. If you can't pay the loan, he or she can take your security and sell it to satisfy the debt!

In order to be eligible for a personal loan, you will usually have to have a full- or part-time job, a good history of payment of previous loans, and *something of value* that the lender can use to pay off the loan if you can't meet the payments. That "something of value" is called *collateral.*

Since the personal loan is the cheapest way to borrow money, it's worth trying to get one before settling for an installment sales contract.

Shopping for a Loan

Installment loan contracts (personal loans) are offered by commercial banks, savings and loan institutions, credit unions, and finance companies. Installment sales contracts are also offered by these institutions and by stores and automobile dealers.

In general, no matter which type of loan you want, a credit union will give you the least expensive loan, followed by savings and loans, banks, large stores, and automobile dealers. Small stores, dealers, and finance companies are the most expensive.

One easy way to find out what a loan will cost is to call a number of potential lenders. Explain to each one how much money you want to borrow, what you intend to do with it, and how long a repayment period you would like. Then ask:

- What is the annual percentage rate (APR)? Note that the APR is the yearly interest you pay on the loan. The lower the interest, the lower your cost. Look for the *lowest* APR you can find.
- What is the monthly payment?
- What is the total cost of the loan, including all service charges?

The answers you get will tell you where to borrow money, and you'll then be ready to look at the contract you'll be asked to sign.

What a Contract Is and What It Must Contain

An installment contract is a legal document that delineates your rights and responsibilities and those of the lender. Your contract will be a preprinted form with blanks that must be filled in. The contract was written by a lawyer and designed to favor the lender, so it's very important to understand it before you sign it. By law the following information must appear on the contract:

EXAMPLE

Brief description of item purchased	1976 car
Price	$2,100.00
Less down payment	$ 100.00
Plus insurance on loan	$ 42.00
Total amount financed	$2,042.00
Finance charge	$ 877.04
Annual percentage rate (APR)	18%
Number of payments	24
When due	1st of month
Total payments of loan	$2,919.12

If you forget everything else in this chapter, you can still keep out of trouble if you read the following hints carefully before you make a purchase.

Most merchants and businesses are honest, reputable institutions that will not try to cheat you. Even honest merchants, however, use contract forms that are slanted in their favor. The following points will help you when you're about to sign *any* contract.

Before You Sign Any Contract

- Don't borrow more than you can afford.
- *Read and understand* all of your contract before you sign it. Ascertain that the points mentioned on page 80 are included. Be sure that the APR shown in the contract is the same one quoted to you.
- Make sure all the blank spaces in the contract are filled in so they can't be filled in afterwards.
- If you don't understand it, take a filled-in, but unsigned, contract home overnight and have a friend or lawyer explain it to you. This is legal. *Beware* of the seller who doesn't want you to take the contract home.
- If changes are made in the contract, make sure both you and the seller initial them.
- Be sure your copy is the same as the seller's.
- If the seller makes any promises, be sure they are written down in the contract.
- If you are asked to be a cosigner on someone else's loan, you should be aware that you must pay the debt if the other person doesn't make the payments. Be choosy!

Warnings

- If your contract contains the words "waive" or "waiver," watch out! These words require you to give up one of your rights. You'll need a clear explanation from a responsible person as to what you are being asked to give up.
- Watch out for "balloon payments." This means that one of your payments will be quite a bit larger than the rest. It is usually the last payment. You will pay a lot of extra interest and you may have trouble making the last large payment.
- Every loan contract contains some method of penalizing you

for late or missed payments. Watch out for the following methods:

1. Loan contracts that state that the entire loan becomes due and payable immediately if you are late or miss a payment—and at the same time *you* pay any collection fees.
2. Loan contracts that give the lender the authority to ask your employer to deduct some or all of the missed payments from your pay check.
3. Loan contracts that require an unreasonably high "late charge."

• Be cautious of a merchant who does not offer credit himself, but offers you application forms from some other lender. Such a merchant usually doesn't have enough capital to extend loans, so he or she uses a finance company. Not only are the finance charges higher under this arrangement, but you could find yourself having to pay installments to a finance company for goods that were broken or never delivered.

OVERDUE BILLS

If you find that you are having difficulty meeting the payment on your debts, don't panic. Here are some tips that could help.

Credit-Counseling Services

The safest and cheapest way to get help is to consult the Consumer Credit Counseling Services of your state or local government. These are usually free professional money-management services. To locate the one nearest you, call your local Consumer Protection Agency or write:

National Foundation for Consumer Credit
1819 H Street NW
Washington, D.C. 20006

The advice you receive from these agencies can be trusted.

Debt Consolidation Loans

You often see advertisements for debt consolidation loans. This type of loan is an expensive way to get out of your difficulties. Avoid it.

Debt Collectors

There are new laws that prevent debt-collection agencies from abusing you while they are trying to collect a debt. Contact the Federal Trade Commission if you feel you are being abused by any collection agency.

CREDIT RECORDS

Once you start using credit, credit records will be kept on you. These records, kept by credit bureau companies, tell how well you pay bills. The Fair Credit-Reporting Act provides that you can obtain a copy of your credit record. Call your bank or other lender for the name of the credit bureau it uses. Then write or phone for a copy of your report. Remember that a bad credit record can't haunt you forever. If the report contains a bad credit rating and you would like to tell your side of the dispute, contact the credit bureau and ask how to enter your side of the story into their records. Credit bureaus normally have forms for that purpose.

Information on a bad debt must be removed from your credit record after seven years, and bankruptcy information must be removed after fourteen years.

7 | Insurance

The concept of insurance sometimes seems foreign to us during our younger years.

"I'm a good driver," we might think. "I'm not going to hit anyone."

"I've never been sick a day in my life."

"Accidents happen to other people."

There's some truth in each of these statements, but once you're out from under the protective wing of someone else's insurance plan, you run many risks if you don't have insurance! One young man had a two-and-a-half-year-old compact car worth $3,100. He let the insurance lapse because he wanted to spend the money for something else. Then his car was totaled by another driver who had no insurance. Result: he got $35 from the scrap dealer. There are thousands of such stories, and I recommend that we look at the types of insurance available so you can decide which kind is best for you.

Insurance provides financial protection from all types of disasters. When you buy an insurance policy, you are normally covered from the moment you make the first payment. There are exceptions to this, however. Some policies, primarily medical insurance, require a *waiting period* before you receive benefits. If you miss a payment, most states allow a thirty- to thirty-one-day "grace period." That means that you are covered under the insurance policy for thirty to thirty-one days after your last payment was due. Other state laws may *not* have the standard "grace period." *Ask* your agent, to make sure you know what you're getting. The types of insurance we will discuss are Life, Auto, Medical/Health, and Renters'.

TERMS YOU SHOULD KNOW

Here are some basic insurance terms and a short explanation of each:

AUTO INSURANCE: provides money to cover damages you have caused with your car, as well as those done to you.

BENEFICIARY: the person who will receive the money from a life insurance policy.

CASH VALUE: money on *certain* life insurance policies that accrues, or builds up, and will be returned when the policy is cashed in.

CONVERTIBLE: a type of policy that can be changed from one kind to another (example: term insurance converts to life).

COVERAGE: all the risks or circumstances that the insurance policy includes.

DEDUCTIBLE: the amount of money you must pay in case of an accident or illness ($50 deductible means that you pay the first $50 of the cost and the insurance company pays the rest up to the amount you are insured for).

DEPENDENTS: family members or others whom you want to provide for.

DIVIDEND: a payment made to you if you are a member of a mutual insurance company and there are profits (special insurance).

EXCLUSIONS: risks that are *not* covered by the insurance policy.

INSURANCE AGENT: a person who works for one insurance company only.

INSURANCE BROKER: a person who represents many companies and can offer the best coverage for your needs.

LIABILITY: responsibility.

LIFE INSURANCE: protects you from financial problems caused by a death in a family. The head of the household is usually the one insured.

MEDICAL OR HEALTH INSURANCE: protects you from the financial burden of accident or illness to yourself or your family.

POLICY: the contract you sign with the insurance company.

PREMIUM: the amount of money you pay for insurance.

RIDERS: clauses adding coverage for risks not normally covered by the policy.

15/30/5: minimum auto-liability coverage required by law. The "15" means that a single person can collect up to $15,000 for bodily injuries in one accident. The "30" means that $30,000 is the most the insurance company will pay for one accident. The "5" means that $5,000 is the most an insurance company will pay in property damages for one accident.

Now we'll explain the three main types of insurance.

LIFE INSURANCE

It seems that a life insurance salesperson will try to sell you a policy at least three times a year. Remember, he's convinced that he's doing you a favor, that you really need the insurance, and that his company's policy is the best one for you. Because you'll sooner or later face the situation, it's a good idea to decide beforehand whether or not you want to buy. In general, if no one depends on you for support, there will be no pressing need to have life insurance. If you're married, and particularly if you have children, you should seriously consider it.

A life insurance policy is a contract that guarantees a certain sum of money will be paid to the beneficiary of your choice if you die while the policy is in effect. In most cases the "breadwinner" in the family is the person who is insured.

There are two basic types of life insurance: "term" and "whole," or "straight."

Term Insurance

This is the simplest form of life insurance. For a certain length of time, usually five years, you pay a premium that guarantees a specified amount of money will be paid to your beneficiary if you die during that term or period. At the end of the term you may renew the policy, but your premium will cost more because as you grow older you are more likely to die. The advantage of term insurance is that it costs less and provides higher benefits while you are young.

Whole, or Straight Life, Insurance

The most popular type of coverage, whole life insurance does not have to be renewed because its coverage never runs out if you make your payments on time; and your payments never go up. A cash value accrues if you decide to cash in your policy while you are alive. If you die, the cash value disappears into the company profits, but your beneficiary receives the money specified by the insurance policy. For instance, you have a $5,000 policy with a cash value of $500. If you die, your beneficiary receives only $5,000. The $500 goes back to the company.

A limited type of whole life is also available. You pay high premiums for a limited time, and then you are covered for life. This policy is especially good for athletes or people with limited high-earning years.

Tips Concerning Life Insurance

- A young person needs only term insurance.
- The amount of life insurance you should have is usually five times your annual salary (example: $10,000 salary, $50,000 insurance).
- Look for insurance companies that offer policies that can be *converted* from one type to another.
- You can combine types of policies to get what is best for you.
- *Group insurance* from your employer is much cheaper (a big savings).
- You can become a member of some insurance companies by paying a higher premium. Then, if the company has a good year, you will receive a cash dividend.
- Borrowing on a life insurance policy is often confusing. If you borrow $2,000 on a $5,000 policy you pay a lower rate of interest on your loan, but your insurance coverage is lowered to $3,000 until the loan is paid back.

AUTOMOBILE INSURANCE

Automobile insurance covers damage you've caused with your car as well as damage done to you. Automobile insurance is made up of five parts: liability coverage, comprehensive, collision, uninsured motorist, and medical-payment provisions.

Liability Coverage

This type of insurance takes care of damages you cause. Minimum coverage is 15/30/5.

The amount of coverage you want depends on you, but don't shortchange yourself on liability coverage. The minimum 15/30/5 can be increased to 50/100/25 for a few extra dollars a year. Medical costs are so high that you need a good deal of liability coverage.

In some states the law requires that automobile owners carry minimum liability coverage. If you break the law and attempt to drive without the minimum coverage, you may be fined and have your license suspended for three years.

Comprehensive

This covers damages *to your car* that are not caused by auto collision or mechanical problems. You are protected from damages due to falling objects, fire, vandalism, riot, theft, water, animal collision, glass breakage, earthquake, and other causes. The cost of comprehensive coverage varies from city to city, depending on car-theft and weather patterns.

Collision

Damages to *your* car are covered in cases of collision regardless of who is responsible for the accident. Your insurance company pays for the damages immediately, and you will not have to wait for a long settlement. The cost of collision insurance depends on the year, make, and model of your car. If you have an accident, the insurance company's settlement with you will be based on the current value of your car. Therefore, as your car gets older this kind of insurance is less important. If your car is worth less than $1,000, it may not pay to carry collision. Comprehensive and collision insurance are *not* required by law.

Uninsured Motorist

This insurance covers you if you have an accident with a driver who is not insured or with a hit-and-run driver. Your compensation is what it would be if the other driver carried the minimum coverage (15/30/5) to pay you or your passengers for injuries.

Medical Payment

Medical expenses for you and your passengers are provided if an accident occurs. Medical coverage protects you from liability for your passenger's medical bills.

Cost Factors

You may be interested in the factors that influence the cost of auto insurance.

- Driving records: These are kept for three years. Insurance rates are higher for those who have moving violations or accidents during the three-year period. Insurance companies may refuse to insure anyone with too many violations.
- Sex and age: Men between the ages of eighteen and twenty-five pay the highest rates. Rates are reduced for single men over twenty-seven. Rates for married men go down when they reach twenty-five. Single women's rates are reduced when they are twenty-one. Married women's rates are based on the husband's age.
- Use of car: Pleasure drivers pay the lowest rates. Drivers who use their cars for business pay the highest rates. The greater the distance traveled, the more insurance will cost.
- Residence: City premiums are higher than those of other areas. Rates in high-crime areas are highest.
- Type of car: Insurance on new sports cars is the most expensive. It also costs more for larger cars than for smaller cars, and for newer cars than for older cars.

After you have decided what coverage you need, it is a good idea to phone some brokers and get prices. If they refuse to quote prices hang up and try others who will. Be sure to ask about good-student discounts or nondrinkers' discounts. Also *ask* what other discounts are available.

No-Fault Auto Insurance

About half of the states have enacted legislation to allow "no-fault" auto insurance. The concept is simple. Each person's damages are paid for by his own or her own insurance company, regardless of who caused the accident. Each state has different rules about payment limits for various types of medical treatment, and some do not allow lawsuits. To find out about the regulations in your state, call or write its Department of Insurance.

Tips for Buying Auto Insurance

- Be sure the agent or insurance company is *trustworthy*. Ask friends and relatives about their experiences with different companies. You might pay a lower price in some companies, but they may not be very good at paying their claims. We have had this experience with a leading insurer.

- Ask your librarian for the July 1977 *Consumer's Report*. The magazine polled its readers and asked them to rate their insurance companies according to how they paid their claims.
- It might be better to do business with an insurance broker rather than an insurance agent. The broker represents a number of different companies and may give better deals than an agent who is associated with only one company. *Shop around.*
- It is cheaper to pay your premiums yearly than to pay monthly or quarterly.
- Deductibles keep auto-insurance rates lower. The higher the deductible, the lower your payments. If you have an accident and carry a $300 deductible policy, you would have to pay the first $300. But you can deduct all but the first $100 of your uninsured loss from your net income on your income tax return. It works like this:

> $300 deductible
> − 100 not allowed by tax law
>
> $200 loss can be deducted from your net income on your tax return if you itemize your deductions.

- Ask what discounts are available to you.
- Increase your liability if you can afford it, and consider dropping your collision and comprehensive if your car's value is less than $1,000.

HEALTH INSURANCE

Health insurance is very important, especially in these days of rapidly rising medical costs. Find some way to obtain coverage under an adequate individual or group plan. The five main types of health insurance are discussed below.

Hospital/Medical/Surgical

This type of coverage is the basic health plan. The policy covers room charges, doctors' and surgeons' fees, and most other services. Some policies pay the full cost of health care; others pay only dollar amounts or percentages of the total cost. Most accidents or illnesses that require hospital care are included in this coverage. However, doctor's office visits and house calls generally are not.

Major Medical

This is a back-up policy for serious accidents or illness. It picks up where basic coverage ends. It can include such services as drugs, blood, and therapy. Frequently major-medical plans have a deductible and the policy pays all costs up to the limit of coverage. This coverage may offer benefits as high as $25,000 to $50,000. However, since the chances of a major accident or illness are relatively small, this extra coverage is inexpensive.

Comprehensive Health Coverage

This combines the benefits of Hospital/Medical/Surgical and Major Medical coverage. Most group plans fall under this category.

Supplemental

This coverage is an addition to other coverage. Supplemental generally is purchased to cover hospital confinement or an extensive illness such as cancer.

Prepaid Health Plan

This plan requires that you pay a monthly charge whether you are sick or not. If you become ill, everything from a doctor's visit to major surgery costs about a one-dollar registration fee. Be sure to look into such plans. Check the telephone book under "Health Maintenance Organizations" (HMO).

One of the usual ways of buying medical insurance is through a group health plan. Your employer may offer a group plan as one benefit. Group plans are usually less expensive and include more services than individual policies.

Prepaid Health Plan Complaints

Usually the individual plan has a grievance committee. If you do not receive satisfaction there, write to your state Department of Corporations. Sometimes your state Health Department can be of help in medical insurance problems. (See also "Emergency Help" in Chapter 10.)

Nongroup Policies

If you must carry an individual policy, here are some questions the California Department of Consumer Affairs recommends you ask your health insurance agent:

- Is the insurance company licensed in your state? (Call the state Department of Insurance.)
- What types of service benefits are covered? Does your policy include diagnostic tests, prescription drugs, out-patient care, private-duty nursing?
- Does your policy cover both illness and accidents? What types of illnesses and accidents are covered? Which exclusions limit your coverage?
- Does the policy offer the full amount, a certain percentage of the amount, *or* only dollar amounts? Some policies offer 80 percent coverage for drugs. Others will pay up to a specific amount, such as $100. Should you need expensive, prolonged drug treatment, $100 will be insufficient. Dollar amounts are often unreliable, as costs vary widely from place to place.
- Does the policy stipulate a waiting period during which all or certain illnesses are not covered? The shorter the waiting period and the more illnesses covered, the better off you are.
- Does the policy exclude coverage for preexisting conditions for a certain period of time? Most policies have two-year exclusion clauses, and exclusion clauses up to three years are legal. Naturally, the shorter the time period, the better.
- What are the permanent exclusions? Almost all policies have some, including drug addiction and alcoholism.
- Does the policy include maternity coverage? You must often wait a specified period of time from the effective date of your policy before maternity benefits will be covered. This waiting period should be no longer than nine or ten months.
- Can your policy be canceled by the insurance company? If so, under what circumstances? Under what circumstances can your premium be raised?

Mail-Order Health Insurance

There are some mail-order health insurers who have not established very good records of claims payment. A United States Senate committee reported that one major mail-order company rejected 38.5 percent of its claims in one year. So be careful. Be sure to look for the exact coverages, exclusions, and riders.

RENTERS' INSURANCE

When you are first setting up an apartment, you may not give a thought to renters' insurance. But think for a moment. How much will it cost to replace that stereo and record collection? How about the TV, your clothes, furniture, jewelry, and so on? Your landlord's insurance will probably cover damage to the building but not damage or theft of your personal property. For an annual fee of between $38 to $100 you can be insured against fire or theft and many other hazards as well. These include damage from vandalism, storms, lightning, aircraft, and other causes.

Renters' insurance covers both personal property damage and, for an additional fee, "personal liability" for accidents that might happen in or out of your apartment. Discuss all of the available options with at least two or three insurance brokers to be sure you are getting the best coverage for the least money.

Tips on Renters' Insurance

- Consider carefully the cost of replacing your belongings and how much you can afford to pay for insurance.
- Be realistic in assessing the value of your property. Some insurance companies may even require photos of your expensive belongings.
- Make a list of your personal property and keep it in a safe place *outside* of the apartment (parents' or friend's home, or safety deposit box) so that if there is a fire or theft you will have an accurate account of your losses.
- Shop for the best coverage. Look for an insurance company that offers to pay for the actual cost of replacing the lost or damaged goods without deducting wear and tear or depreciation.

  Ask if there are discounts available. For example, some companies give discounts on policies if you have smoke or fire alarms.
- Be sure that you understand the policy completely before you sign for it. Check for any "waivers," "exceptions," or "exclusions," in your policy and have them explained to your satisfaction.

PROBLEMS WITH YOUR INSURANCE POLICY

If you feel that your insurance company has not lived up to its agreement, contact the Policy Services Bureau in your state. Include the following information in your *written* report. The insurance department usually will not handle complaints over the phone.

* Name and address of insurance company
* Your policy number or claim number, or a *copy* of the policy if possible
* A brief statement of the facts. Try to be accurate about names, dates, and places.
* *Copies* of receipts or information that will help your claim

Your state Insurance Department usually lets you know it has received your complaint in about ten days and completes its report in about sixty days. It cannot order an insurance company to pay a claim, but if an insurance company is found guilty of several violations, its license can be suspended. After the first written complaint, keep up to date on the case by phone.

8 | Clothing

For some, the size of their wardrobe may be dictated by the capacity of their backpack, but if you have a closet, it's good to know how to fill it and still have some money left over to pay the rent.

BASIC RULES

A good rule for the basic wardrobe is the "one-two-three rule": one on your back, one in the drawer, one in the laundry.

Your first concern should be proper dress for work. If you have a job in an office or store, your employer will impose certain dress codes. Try to get at least three changes of such clothes, or you'll have to do a laundry every day. Outside work requires sturdier clothes and at least four or five changes. Remember, the more clothes you have, the more time and energy it takes for upkeep.

Since your clothing budget is limited, it is wise to know what styles and colors look best on you and to buy with this in mind. Three coordinating colors can give you a wide selection of mix-and-match outfits. Start with simple basic styles and add accessories to make different outfits.

Very few people have perfect bodies, so it pays to know some of the techniques fashion designers use to accent positive features and conceal shortcomings. You'll find dozens of helpful hints in fashion magazines, so I'll make only a few basic suggestions here.

Hints for Women

If you have a good figure, you can wear anything. If not, here are a few pointers:

- Tall and underweight: Use horizontal lines or stripes; soft, fluffy styles; textured or heavy fashions; light, warm colors; and contrasting colors in blouses and skirts.
- Short and underweight: Wear soft, fluffy styles; textured heavy fashions; light, warm colors, and prints.
- Tall and overweight: Close-set vertical lines or stripes give the impression of slenderness. Wear basic, simple styles; smooth, nonclinging fashions; and darker colors.
- Short and overweight: Close-set vertical lines or stripes will make you look slender. One solid color gives the illusion of height. Wear soft, nonclinging fabrics in dark colors.
- Big hips: Avoid jackets, belts, or other details that end at the hipline.
- Big bosom: Avoid sleeves that end at the bustline.

Basic Wardrobe

These items of clothing are considered essential:

    1 dress
    1 jumper
    3 blouses (choose blouses that look good with skirts, jumpers, and slacks)
    1 pair of shorts
    2 skirts (should match blouses)
    6 sets of underwear
    1 sweater
    1 pair of dress shoes
    1 pair of sport shoes
    1 jacket
    2 pairs of slacks
    2 pairs of jeans
    1 belt
    1 pair of thongs
    1 coat
    1 pair of gloves
    3 pairs of socks or panty hose
    1 scarf or hat

Remember, one pair of white and one pair of black slacks go with anything.

As you can afford it, add scarves, hats, jewelry, and other accessories.

Hints for Men

- Overweight: Wear smooth-textured materials (no tweeds); dark solid colors; close-set stripes or small patterns; easy-fitting clothes; and pockets without flaps. Avoid short-spread collars and bow ties.
- Underweight: Use tweed or bulky materials; bold patterns, especially plaids; easy-fitting clothes; pockets with flaps; wide-spread collars.
- Tall: Avoid short jackets.
- Short: Wear vertical lines or stripes and long, pointed collars. Avoid double-breasted jackets. The jacket should just cover the seat of the pants. This gives a longer look to the legs.

Basic Wardrobe

3 pairs of jeans (more if work requires them)
3 pairs of slacks (if job requires)
3 T-shirts (optional)
6 pairs of underwear
6 pairs of socks
1 pair of dress shoes
1 pair of sport shoes
1 pair of thongs
1 jacket
1 coat
1 pair of gloves
1 tie for special occasions (3, if job requires)
1 dress shirt (or more)
1 sweater
3 sport shirts
1 belt
1 scarf or hat

Have one drip-dry white dress shirt for emergencies when you have to look nice but don't have time for the laundry.

How to Buy Quality Clothing

Here are some tips for buying clothing of good quality. Some of the clothes in your price range won't have all of these features, but it's worth looking for them, especially in work clothes. Look for:

* Good fabrics (see the fabric chart in this chapter)
* Seams that are wide and smooth, with even, close stitching
* Hems that are even and deep enough to lengthen if necessary
* Buttonholes that are neat, strong, and sewn on both sides
* Double stitching in areas that tear easily
* Zippers that are smooth and carefully sewn
* Lines in plaid or striped materials that match at the seams and at the buttons

Fabrics

To put together a basic wardrobe, it helps to know a little about fabrics and how to clean them. The best source of information is the manufacturer's label on the back of the garment. This should tell you the type of fabric and how to clean it. The chart on page 100 lists the most common types of fabrics used today and some helpful information about each. Remember that "permaprest" is easiest. If the label reads "50 percent cotton, 50 percent polyester," or "35 percent polyester, 65 percent cotton," the garment will wash and dry well.

HOW TO CUT CLOTHING COSTS

When your budget is limited, it's good to know how expert bargain hunters shop. The first rule is to *buy basics.* The second is to *shop.* When buying garments on sale, make sure they fit, because most sale items can't be returned. Watch your newspaper or ask the salesperson in the store when the next sale will be held. Most stores schedule their sales like this:

Women's coats: April, August, November, December
Dresses: January, April, June, November
Lingerie: January, May, July
Men's coats: January, August
Men's shirts: January, February, July
Men's suits: April, November, December

Sportswear: January, February, May, July
Shoes: January, July, November, December

Tips on Sales

Ask to be placed on the store's mailing list. You'll receive advance notice and may be invited to sales before the general public. Avoid spending a lot of money on fad fashions. Remember gaucho pants and Nehru jackets? Do *not* buy on impulse! Plan *all* of your purchases. If you see something you can't live without, try asking the salesperson to hold it for you for twenty-four hours. You may decide that you don't need it after all.

Thrift Shops

Last spring, my husband had to take a business trip to Europe, and I was able to go with him. April in Paris! We anticipated basking in warm spring-time sunshine and chose our clothes accordingly. Surprise! We got rain in London, Paris, and Venice; snow in Germany; and temperatures much too cold for our thin Phoenix blood everywhere we went. The first stop for my husband was in the lovely southwestern coastal area of England, while I toured London and waited for him to rejoin me. Since he had refused to bring a topcoat, I decided to buy him a coat. I won't tell you how much they wanted at Harrod's for an ordinary tan raincoat with a zip-in lining, but even at the less-expensive stores in Picadilly Circus, there was nothing under $150.00.

I had to start skimping immediately if I was going to pull that much out of my mad money. That same afternoon I bundled up our soiled laundry and looked for a laundromat. Next door to the laundromat was a thrift shop, and in the window was a serviceable tan raincoat with a zip-in lining! It cost $6.00 and was a bit too big, but it kept him warm, and when we got back to Phoenix, we recycled it—right into the nearest thrift box.

Thrift shops are excellent for bargain hunters, but be choosy! Some are loaded with junk, while others have quality clothes at unbelievably low prices. Walk through a number of thrift shops before you decide where to buy. The same rules apply to shopping in thrift shops as in department stores, with a few differences. There may not be a label to check, so look carefully at seams and other points of stress. Make sure the underarms and crotches are not torn or soiled. Most thrift shops do not sell

Material	Good Features
Cotton	• strong yet soft and comfortable • color fast, heat resistant • may be mercerized (treated to strengthen the fiber and add luster) • may be sanforized (less than 1% shrinkage) • may be preshrunk (less than 3% shrinkage)
Wool	• warm • strong, absorbent, colorfast • resists wrinkling • does not burn easily and is self extinguishing
Rayon	• soft, comfortable • absorbent, colorfast

Bad Features	Care
• shrinks unless sanforized or preshrunk • burns easily unless treated by manufacturer • holds creases poorly unless blended with polyester	• hand washing: warm or cold water • machine washing: hot, warm, or cold water • machine drying: any cycle • drip drying: clothesline or coat hanger • dry cleaning: optional • bleach: optional • detergent: strong, medium, or mild • ironing: medium or high heat
• shrinks in warm or hot water • forms small, fuzzy balls (pills) • poor resistance to moths	• hand washing: lukewarm or cold water • machine washing: never • machine drying: never • drip drying: lay flat and stretch to shape • dry cleaning: best method of cleaning • bleach: never • detergent: mild • ironing: low heat
• not very strong • wrinkles easily • mildews easily • burns easily unless treated by manufacturer	• hand washing: warm water • machine washing: never • machine drying: delicate fabric cycle • drip drying: clothesline or coat hanger • dry cleaning: optional (see label) • bleach: never • detergent: mild • ironing: medium heat

Material	Good Features
Polyester	• strong, colorfast • resists wrinkling and creasing • blend of cotton and polyester combines the best characteristics of both
Acrylic	• resembles wool • colorfast • resists mildew • holds crease, resists wrinkles • warm • sun resistant
Nylon	• very strong • good shape retention • somewhat elastic

Bad Features	Care
• pills • not absorbent • attracts lint • melts under high heat	• hand washing: warm or cold water • machine washing: warm water • machine drying: any cycle (use antistatic product) • drip drying: clothesline, coat hanger, or flat • dry cleaning: optional • bleach: optional • detergent: any • ironing: not required (use medium heat for touch-up)
• pills • not strong • not absorbent • holds static • burns readily	• hand washing: warm water • machine washing: warm water • machine drying: delicate cycle • drip drying: never • dry cleaning: optional (see label) • bleach: optional • detergent: any • ironing: medium setting
• wrinkles easily, pills • not absorbent • fades in sunlight • burns and melts under high heat	• hand washing: warm water • machine washing: warm water • machine drying: delicate fabric cycle • drip drying: coat hanger • dry cleaning: not necessary • bleach: optional • detergent: any • ironing: medium heat

Material	Good Features
Acetate	• looks like silk • can be either soft or crisp • resists mildew
Silk	• fairly strong • absorbent • colorfast • wrinkle resistant • does not burn easily
Spandex (almost always combined with other fabrics)	• very elastic • resists body oils • resists cosmetics • resists sunlight

Bad Features	*Care*
• wrinkles easily • not absorbent • does not wash well • melts with high heat	• hand washing: warm water • machine washing: never • machine drying: never • drip drying: clothesline or coat hanger • dry cleaning: optional (see label) • bleach: never • detergent: mild or medium • ironing: low heat
• expensive • weakened by heat • can be yellowed by age, sunlight, or strong soap • poor crease retention	• hand washing: warm or cool water • machine washing: never • machine drying: never • drip drying: clothesline or coat hanger • dry cleaning: preferred cleaning method • bleach: never • detergent: mild • ironing: low heat
• yellows with age • melts under high heat	• hand washing: warm water • machine washing: warm water • machine drying: delicate fabric cycle • drip drying: clothesline or coat hanger • dry cleaning: optional (see label) • bleach: never • detergent: mild • ironing: not required

soiled clothes, but check. All sales are final, so be sure you want whatever you buy.

To find thrift shops, check your Yellow Pages under "Second-hand Stores." Also, your local bookstore may have a bargain-hunters' guide, listing addresses, phone numbers, approximate prices, hours, and other information for thrift shops in your area.

Factory Outlets

Factory outlets are listed in your Yellow Pages under "Women's Apparel—Wholesale and Manufacturers" and under "Men's Clothing—Wholesale and Manufacturers." They can also be found in local bargain-hunters' guides. Factory outlets often sell seconds. Watch for mis-sizing, bad coloring, sewing defects, fabric defects, and mended tears. Many articles of clothing are worth buying, but look them over very carefully.

Catalog Shopping

Ordering from a catalog can save time, money, and the wear and tear of shopping. Know the reputation of the catalog house and what its return policy is.

Sell Your Used Clothes

Your thrift shop may sell them for you, or you can sell them in garage sales or just swap them among your friends. Happy hunting!

9 | Health and Fitness

Someone once asked Ingrid Bergman her recipe for a long and happy life. Her response: "Good health and a bad memory."

She confessed that she had stolen the line from Claudette Colbert, and when she had a chance to tell Claudette about it, that gracious lady said: "You're welcome to it. I stole it from Albert Schweitzer!"

It's a good line no matter where it originated. And it's my wish for you. Good health to enjoy the pleasant times, and a bad memory to forget the unpleasant.

MEDICAL CARE

Types of Doctors

Medical doctors are divided into primary-care doctors and specialists. The primary-care doctor performs routine health-care and physical check-ups. If something more serious develops he may refer you to a specialist.

The primary-care doctors are known as general practitioners, or GPs. Some doctors specialize in primary care, and these specialists are called family doctors, or internists.

A specialist does not have to have extra training, but in order to be a *board-certified specialist,* he or she must have extra training and must pass a difficult exam given by the American Medical Board. To find out about your doctor, ask your local medical society, listed in the Yellow Pages under "Physicians." They will describe his or her training and tell you whether he or she is board certified. If they don't mention board certification, ask. You can also check this in the *Directory of Medical Specialists* at your local library.

Since there are so many medical specialists, the following list may help:

Type of Doctor	*Specialty*
allergist	allergies
anesthesiologist	general and local anesthetics
cardiologist	heart and blood vessels
dermatologist	skin and its disorders
family doctor	general health care and check-ups
internist	internal medicine and general health
gynecologist	female reproductive and sexual organs
obstetrician	pregnancy and childbirth
ophthalmologist	eyes, optic nerves
orthopedist	bones and sometimes joints
otolaryngologist	ears, throat, and sometimes nose
pathologist	diseases and their bodily effects
podiatrist	feet
proctologist	rectum, colon (large intestine) and anus
psychiatrist	emotional illness and mental disorders
radiologist	diagnoses and treatment of injury and disease by X rays, and radioactive chemicals and substances
surgeon	operates to correct various injuries, disorders, and diseases (one surgeon does not perform all types of operations; they specialize)

Type of Doctor	*Specialty*
urologist	male and female urinary tract, and male reproductive tract

Choosing a Doctor

There is no hard-and-fast rule to guarantee that you will find a good doctor, but the following may help.

- Ask friends, relatives, or someone connected with the medical field, like a nurse.
- If you are moving, ask your present doctor to recommend a doctor in your new town.
- Check the *Directory of Medical Specialists* in your library for board-certified doctors in the specialty you need.
- Your local county medical society keeps a list of all the doctors and surgeons in the country who are members of the society. They will give you the names of several doctors, depending on your needs and residence. The names are given on a rotating basis, and you should be sure to ask if the doctors are *board certified.*

Hospitals

Just as doctors should be licensed and board certified, hospitals should be accredited. An accredited hospital must meet basic standards required by the Joint Commission of Accreditation of Hospitals (JCAH). Most hospitals are accredited, but ask your doctor or check the *Guide to the Health Care Field* in your library.

If You Can't Afford a Private Doctor

- State health department: Many states provide free or low-cost clinics that are run by the Department of Health. These clinics offer pregnancy tests, birth-control devices, and family-planning counseling. They also provide help for venereal disease, alcoholism, and drug abuse. The Department of Health can be found in the white pages of the telephone book under the name of your state.
- Hospital out-patient department: You can go to any hospital that has an out-patient department when you need medical help. Try to find an out-patient clinic that is connected to a

medical school. Teaching hospitals are noted for quality medical care. It may be wise to call for an appointment. Out-patient clinics are not free, but the cost is normally much lower than a visit to a doctor's office.

Surgery

If you are told that you need surgery and it is not emergency surgery, get a second opinion. Go to another doctor and find out whether he or she agrees that the surgery should be performed. This prevents a lot of unnecessary surgery. No good doctor will be upset if you obtain a second opinion. If one doctor says yes and another says no, the final decision will be yours. If you do have the operation, make sure it's performed in an accredited hospital! The government has set up a hot line to help you get a second opinion. The number is 1-800-325-6400.

Prescriptions

Many remedies can be bought "over the counter" at any drugstore. Certain medicines and drugs, however, are controlled by the government because their use without a doctor's supervision can be dangerous or fatal. If your doctor determines that you need one of these controlled substances, he or she will write a prescription for it. Ask your doctor to prescribe a generic drug, rather than a brand-name drug, because generic drugs cost about half as much.

When drug manufacturers invest in the development of a new drug, they get a patent on it. For the period of time covered by the patent, it can be sold only under their brand name and they are the only ones who can manufacture it. This allows them to ask a high price for it to recoup the cost of development.

When the patent runs out, other drug manufacturers are free to make and market the substance. It's the same drug, manufactured with adequate quality control, but it can't be called by the same name that the original manufacturer gave it. Therefore it's called a generic drug. Even if your doctor doesn't prescribe generic drugs, some states allow druggists to dispense the cheaper generic drug as a substitute, but only if you *ask*!

Problems That May Come Up

Your doctor is dedicated to getting you well if you're sick and to keeping you well if you're not sick. Even with the best intentions in the world, both you and your doctor are human, which means that problems or misunderstandings may occur. If you do have a problem with your doctor, be sure to talk it over with him or her personally, not with the office staff. If the problem is of a serious nature that you cannot resolve, mail a written complaint to your local county medical society or contact your local Department of Consumer Affairs. They will refer you to the right agency to help resolve the issue.

DENTAL CARE

Parents, teachers, dentists, and TV commercials have been preaching at us for years to brush our teeth properly. There are lots of good reasons to do so, but the two I like best are that dentists are so expensive and toothaches are so miserable!

Types of Dentists

About 90 percent of all dentists perform regular dental care. The other 10 percent are specialists:

Type of Dentist	Specialty
periodontist	treats gums (means "around teeth")
endodontist	root-canal work (means "in teeth")
pedodontist	treats children
orthodontist	straightens teeth
prosthodontist	does denture work (false teeth)
oral surgeon	surgery and extractions

Choosing a Dentist

If you've moved, you may want to find a dentist in your new neighborhood before you get a toothache. To find a good dentist:

- Ask friends or relatives.
- Ask your doctor. Good doctors usually know who the good dentists are.
- If you live near a dental school, call and ask if any of the teaching staff has a private practice, or if they can refer you to a dentist in the area.

A good dentist's first concern will be to save your teeth, and he or she will do everything possible to avoid pulling them. The dentist will encourage and instruct you in their care. Avoid any dentist that:

* Seems anxious to pull your teeth.
* Finds extensive work to be done; maybe you should seek a second opinion to make sure the work is necessary.
* Doesn't put a lead apron on you when taking X rays.
* Refuses to give you an estimate of the costs.
* Has no emergency telephone numbers.
* Does not explain the treatments or alternatives available.

Check-up X rays should be taken no more than once a year. A full set for check-up purposes should be taken every five years.

If You Can't Afford a Dentist
* Your local hospital may have a dental department.
* Local dental schools have clinics where the students do the work but are closely supervised.
* Your state Health Department might know of private free dental clinics.

Problems That May Come Up
Most problems can be resolved by having a discussion with your dentist. If that doesn't help you can:

* Contact your local American Dental Association. It will try to resolve the problem.
* If you need more help, contact your local Department of Consumer Affairs to find out how to go about finding help.

HEALTH AND EXERCISE

The Basics
Mixed in among the childhood memories we carry with us are certain axioms that represent the wisdom of the ages. Included in these are the oft-repeated comments:

* Brush your teeth! (Brush after every meal.)
* Wash behind your ears! (Use good personal hygiene.)

- Eat your vegetables! (Eat well-balanced meals.)
- Mow the lawn! (Get regular exercise.)
- Don't smoke! (Protect your internal environment.)
- Stay sober! (Keep control of your own actions.)
- Get to bed! (Sleep six to eight hours in each twenty-four.)

When we sort these out, we realize that they lay the pattern for staying healthy and fit.

Even though you may be in good health now, it's important to recognize the symptoms of diseases that may strike. If you are aware of the warning signs, you can contact your doctor early. In most cases, the earlier the treatment, the better your chances of being cured. This is especially true with cancer.

Early Warning Signs of Cancer

The following are the early-warning signals published by the American Cancer Society:

- Change in bowel or in urinary habits
- A sore throat that does not heal
- Unusual bleeding or discharge
- Thickening or lump in breast or elsewhere. All women should learn to give themselves breast examinations. (Check your white pages under "American Cancer Society." They have pamphlets that show you how to check for breast cancer.) Women should also have a Pap test every year.
- Indigestion or difficulty swallowing
- Changes in wart or mole size
- Nagging cough or hoarseness

Remember that these symptoms do not mean you have cancer, and don't become frightened if you notice one. It's not usually serious, but make sure by having it checked right away. The earlier you find out, the better your chances of a cure if it is cancer, and the sooner your mind will be at ease if it is not cancer.

Just by reading your local newspaper you'll learn of many hospitals and health organizations that offer free or very low-cost examinations for cancer, glaucoma, tuberculosis, high blood pressure, flu inoculations, and so on. Most newspapers and radio stations report on such opportunities as a public service. The Health Department of your city or county government will also be glad to tell you where and when such opportunities are available. They are often called "Health Fairs."

Physical Fitness

Perhaps the best and most pleasant way to practice preventative health is to stay physically fit. It's not just a matter of being the correct weight, although that's a part of it. Certainly, Fat Albert, if he ever grows up, will have a number of aches, pains, and medical problems if he drags that mass of weight around for the rest of his life.

Just as important as weight control, though, is the muscle tone of your legs, arms, belly, back, and—most important—heart muscles. Your library has any number of books that describe various fitness programs, but there's one cardinal rule before you start any of them: *Get your doctor's approval!*

Your doctor may know your general health situation well enough to give you a simple okay, but he or she may want to examine you first. Then start slowly, and build up to more vigorous exercises. Each time you exercise, spend about ten minutes doing mild warm-up exercises. And be sure to wind down the same way.

The best exercise is the type that strengthens your cardiovascular system (heart and circulatory system). Any form of exercise that increases your heartbeat, makes you sweat, and causes you to breathe deeply will strengthen your heart and circulation. Exercise at least three times a week for a half hour each time.

Tips on Exercise Programs

If you get hooked on fitness, use some of the splendid books in your library to learn all there is to know about the subject. In the meantime, here are some things our family has learned that may be interesting for you to know:

- Exercise at least three times a week so that your body establishes an exercise routine.
- Running is one of the best all-around exercises. Whether in the form of jogging or playing racquet ball or some other sport, running is good for your whole system.

- Learn where your chafing and blister points are. Then put a little petroleum jelly (such as Vaseline) on them *before* you begin your exercise.
- Don't be reluctant to spend the money to get a good pair of athletic shoes. Fancy exercise suits look pretty, but if your budget is limited, forget the suit and spend the money on shoes.
- When running or jogging, land naturally on your heels, and roll forward to your toes. This will help prevent strains and injuries.
- Treat sprains with ice wrapped in cloth to prevent injuring the skin. Then use an elastic bandage. Elevate the injured part. Treat as soon as you can.
- Water is the best liquid to drink after you exercise.
- Exercise seems to reduce your appetite, so it has a double advantage!
- If exercise doesn't make you breathe hard, it isn't doing you much good. If you want to be super scientific about how hard to exercise, the following formula will help you to figure it out:
  1. Start with the number 220.
  2. Subtract your age.
  3. Take 75 percent of the result (65 percent if you're overweight or smoke a lot).
  4. This is the level of heartbeat you should get to in each exercise session. For example, suppose you're nineteen years old: 220 − 19 = 201; 75 percent of 201 is 150. You should exercise until your heartbeat increases to 150 beats per minute. You don't need to hold your wrist to time your heartbeat. A much easier way is to locate the carotid artery in your neck. Feel for it just below the angle of your jaw. It has a strong beat and is easy to locate. Count the number of beats you feel in six seconds and add a zero to get your heartbeat rate.
- Health spas often offer excellent facilities in which to conduct your exercise program. A warning is in order, however. It's estimated that up to 80 percent of those who join health spas *quit* in four months or less. Be *sure* you've read the contract thoroughly before you sign up. You don't want to continue paying for facilities you're not using!

NUTRITION AND DIET

General Dwight D. Eisenhower had only one rule concerning diet and nutrition, and he had it posted in every mess hall in the Army: TAKE ALL YOU WANT, BUT EAT ALL YOU TAKE!!!!!!
Of course the Army had expert dieticians and nutritionists who carefully planned meals to assure that they were well balanced.

Balanced Meals

No one but you can balance your food values, so I'd like to give you some pointers about nutrition.
We each need a variety of foods to provide energy and good health. There are four main groups of food that, eaten each day, provide a balanced diet. Those groups and the suggested daily serving sizes are shown in the following:

MILK GROUP
cheese, eggs, milk, and milk
    products
adults: 2 servings a day
teens: 4 servings a day
1 serving = 1 cup milk, or
    1½ ounces cheese, or 2
    eggs

MEAT GROUP
Red meat, fish, chicken, dry
    beans, peas, and nuts
adults: 2 servings a day
teens: 2 servings a day
1 serving = 2 ounces meat,
    fish, poultry, or 4 table-
    spoons peanut butter, or 1
    cup cooked beans

FRUITS AND VEGETABLES
all vegetables and fruits

adults: 4 servings a day
teens: 4 servings a day
1 serving = ½ cup (raw or
    cooked), or 1 whole fruit

BREAD AND CEREAL
whole-grain and enriched
    products
adults: 4 servings a day
teens: 4 servings a day
1 serving = 1 slice bread or
    roll, or ½ cup cooked pasta
    or cereal or rice, or 1
    ounce ready-to-eat cereal

Four daily servings in each group—except meat (two are required)—constitute a well-balanced diet.

Some extra tips on nutrition:

- Dry beans, peas, and nuts are vegetable sources of protein. Nutritionists find that to get a complete protein from vegetable sources, you should combine the vegetable protein with a form of animal protein, such as milk, or cheese.
- You need at least one serving of vitamin C a day and at least one food serving of vitamin A three times a week. Good sources of vitamin C are citrus fruits, chili and sweet peppers, potatoes, broccoli, and melons. Good sources of vitamin A are liver, dark green vegetables, red chili peppers, carrots, butter, or margarine.
- Go light on salt, sugar, and saturated fats.
- Eat more fish and chicken instead of red meat.
- Eat lots of vegetables and fruit.

Maintaining the Proper Weight

Despite our best intentions, some of us are unhappy with our weight. A few of us want to add more, but most of us try to lose a few pounds.

The best method of controlling weight is to eat correctly and to faithfully carry out a good exercise program, but it's good to know some of the keys to a successful weight-loss diet.

- Beware of fad diets. There are zillions of them, and many are extremely dangerous. We have a close friend who went on a mix-it-yourself liquid-protein diet. She followed the instructions precisely and began losing those few extra pounds. Three weeks later, she was in the hospital, in a coma, and near death. Her thyroid gland had quit functioning. She's back on her feet now, but she'll be on medication for the rest of her life.
- Continue to eat well-balanced meals. Make sure you're getting the right number of servings from each of the food groups in the chart.
- Get an inexpensive calorie book. In spite of what some say, calories *do* count. If you take in more than you burn off, those extra calories are stored as fat. Here's a handy formula for keeping your weight constant.

If you are a woman aged eighteen to thirty-five, multiply

your weight by 16. If you weigh 120 pounds, a daily average calorie intake of 1,920 (120 × 16) will keep you at that weight. If you are a man aged eighteen to thirty-five, multiply your weight by 19. If you weigh 160 pounds, a daily average calorie intake of 3,040 (160 × 19) will keep you at that weight.

- To lose weight, remember that 3,500 calories represent a pound. If you cut your daily average intake by 250 calories, you should lose a pound every two weeks.

- You can burn off some calories by exercising. The method, just discussed, of figuring the calorie intake necessary to maintain a given weight includes your *normal* exercise pattern. To maintain a given weight through exercise, you must undertake *additional* exercises. Here are some ways to burn off calories:

Activity	Calories per Hour
bicycling	210
walking	210
mowing (power)	250
golf (no cart)	250
bowling	250
swimming ($^1/_4$ mile)	300
walking briskly	300
volleyball	350
table tennis	360
skating	380
water skiing	480
snow skiing	600
racquet ball	600
handball	600
bicycling (fast)	660
running	900

10 | Emergencies

It is never easy to anticipate a disaster or emergency. And it's human to assume that bad things happen to other people. This book wouldn't be complete, however, if it did not at least alert you to some unexpected dangers and prepare you to deal with them. We'll look at two general areas: natural disasters and medical emergencies.

NATURAL DISASTERS

Some natural disasters come with no warning at all. You may receive advisories of others on your local radio or TV station minutes or hours beforehand. These advisories are issued first as "watches," then as "warnings."

For example, a tornado watch means that tornadoes are expected to develop, and you should get ready for the emergency and stay tuned to the radio or TV for further developments. A tornado warning means a tornado has been spotted, and people near it should take cover immediately.

If you live in an area where tornadoes, hurricanes, or other natural disasters occasionally occur, contact your local Red Cross or Civilian Defense for information containing detailed instructions on conditions and safeguards in your area.

General Preparations

Before looking at specific natural disasters, here are some general rules that apply to all of them.

- Don't panic. Think your way through.
- If told to evacuate, do so quickly.
- Put out fires.
- Turn off the main gas, electric, and water pipes.
- Store some water (in the bathtub if necessary).
- Stock food and chlorine bleach (for water purification).
- Have a battery-powered flashlight and radio.
- Fill your car with gasoline if there is time.

These precautions apply to any disaster for which you've been warned. Following are some things to remember if specific disasters occur.

Earthquake

The Hollywood version of an earthquake, with the earth opening up and swallowing everything in sight, is misleading. Actually, the earth shakes and rolls for from to two to four minutes. The most serious threat is from *falling objects,* such as bricks, trees, parts of buildings, and utility poles. Outer walls and front doorways of buildings are the first to fall.

The Alaskan earthquake in 1964 registered more than 8.4 on the Richter scale! It caused one of the worst tidal waves in history. The tide at Whittier, Alaska, was at the one-foot level before the quake, but within two minutes after the first shock, the water in the bay rose to twenty-six feet. The water fell back to normal, but within the next minute it rose to thirty-five feet. The third wave, at about thirty-five feet, hit Whittier's seafront and caused extensive damage. So if you live near the ocean and experience an earthquake, take off for high ground immediately after the quaking stops.

Where you are when an earthquake hits will determine what you should do.

- Indoors: Get under a strong doorway or a strong table or desk pushed up against an inside wall, or in a hallway. Avoid windows or shelves.
- Outdoors: Try to stay out in the open, where nothing can fall on you. Avoid the temptation to run inside. Check for trees, wires, or falling debris.
- In an automobile: Stop and stay in your car. Try to be in the open. The car top should protect you from falling objects.

Tornadoes

Tornadoes pack a powerful wallop in a small area. We've seen towns that had a 200-foot-wide path of pure destruction through them, while homes on each side of the path weren't even touched.

- Indoors: The safest place is the basement, if you have one. Otherwise try to get under something heavy, like a table or desk next to the center wall of the lowest floor of your house. Closets are good places, too. If you have time, open some of the windows to equalize the pressure.
- Outdoors: Remember that tornadoes seldom follow a straight path, and their twists and turns are impossible to predict. If you're caught in the open when a tornado is in the area:
  1. Seek shelter in a strong building (*not* a mobile home or a building with a large flat roof, such as a gymnasium).
  2. If there is no strong building nearby, run at right angles to the funnel. For example, if a tornado approaches from the south, run either east or west.
  3. If you find that you're going to get caught, dive into any ditch or low place, lie flat, and cover your mouth with your shirt or any other cloth to avoid inhaling dust.
- In an automobile: If you're in your car when a tornado approaches, get out of the car and run for shelter.

Hurricanes

Hurricanes are super-giant wind and rain storms that wreak destruction over hundreds of square miles. Their paths are more predictable than those of tornadoes, but they are so immense that if you're in their path, you probably will not be able to get away.

Our family has many hurricane stories, from the big one on Cape Cod that somehow spared our house near the ocean, to the one that almost capsized my husband's aircraft carrier, and finally the one that blew our dog away. We found her two days later, wet and bewildered, and immensely happy to see us. We have learned to respect the big wind called "hurricane" in the Western Hemisphere and "typhoon" in the Eastern.

In coastal areas, flooding usually accompanies hurricanes, so it's wise to know the basic precautions to take in each situation.

- Indoors: When the Weather Service Advisory on your radio or TV channel announces a hurricane watch, get prepared. Close your shutters or board up your windows to avoid flying glass. Tie down or bring in everything that could blow away. Open the windows on the side *opposite* the direction the wind is coming from. Check the list at the beginning of this chapter. When the winds reach their danger point, take shelter at the lowest point of the house, away from walls and windows. The danger is not necessarily over when the wind dies down. Hurricanes spin counterclockwise with tremendous velocity around an "eye" that is relatively calm. Once the eye has passed over, the winds may hit again from the opposite direction. Just to be on the safe side, after the eye has passed, close the open windows and open the opposite ones.

  When the storm is over, check for damage. Turn electricity, water, and gas on *carefully* and check for leaks. Report damage to the proper utility companies. Don't light any matches or fires until you are sure there are no gas leaks.
- Outdoors: Get inside as quickly as possible. If you're too far away from home, seek shelter in the closest sturdy building.
- In an automobile: Park the car and seek shelter. A car is *no* place to be in a hurricane.

Floods

Phoenix is truly desert country. In an average year, the area gets a little less than 6 inches of rain. Contrast that to Alaska's rainfall, 156 inches in a typical year! In the southwestern part of the country, where we live, flash floods are a danger every time there are thundershowers in the mountains. We've learned to stay away from dry washes and to pick camping spots on high ground.

Nothing we've learned could stop last spring's flood, the result of our second "hundred-year" rainfall in twelve years. We got almost a year's worth of rain in a week! All that rain in such a short period may not pose a problem in many areas, but Phoenix is surrounded by mountains. Once the lakes and reservoirs are filled, there is no place for the excess water to go but down to the normally dry Salt River. And it did, with a vengeance! All but two bridges washed out, and the water flowed in a mile-wide swath in some areas, destroying homes, crops, and businesses.

Here are some of the additional precautions we learned to take as a result of our flood:

- If you are asked to evacuate, don't delay. Turn off utilities, put as much on high shelves as you can, and get out. Delay can cost you your life. The force of floodwater is so great that nothing can stand against it. If you're not clear of the area, you and your car or truck will tumble downstream as easily as a matchstick.
- After the floodwaters recede, the greatest danger will be from broken sewage systems. This is a major cause of typhoid fever. Don't reenter the area until it has been cleared by the local health authorities.

Lightning

"Lightning never strikes twice in the same place," is a common, but totally false, statement. A good example of this is the Empire State Building in New York, which lightning has been observed to strike almost fifty times in a recent year.

Scientists can't fully explain the causes of lightning, but the effects of it can be seen in devastating fires and the electrocution of livestock and people.

Lightning almost always accompanies thunderstorms, which are characterized by dark, rolling clouds, sometimes shaped like an anvil.

- Indoors: During a lightning storm, stay away from windows, doors, fireplaces, and items made of metal, such as stoves, sinks, and pipes. Don't use electrical appliances. Because lightning may strike the telephone lines outside, stay off the telephone during the storm. Be sure to unplug your television set.
- Outdoors: Anyone out in the open during thundershower activity is a target for lightning, which hits things that stand higher than their surroundings. Try to get into a building or a car, but if it is impossible to do so, your best protection is a place close to the ground (ditch or cave). Metal and water are excellent conductors of lightning, so avoid anything made of metal and stay away from water during a storm.

If your hair stands on end and your skin feels tingly, crouch down and try to curl into a ball with only your feet touching the ground. You may be about to be hit by lightning. Persons hit by lightning retain no electrical charge and can sometimes be saved with cardiopulmonary resuscitation (CPR).

- In an Automobile: You're very safe in a car. We were driving through a violent thunderstorm a couple of years ago, when our car was hit by lightning. Instead of the harsh glare we might have expected, we were surrounded by a soft rose-tinted light, which lasted for a few seconds. Our rubber tires had effectively insulated the car, and no damage was done.

Blizzards

Blizzards and heavy snowstorms have become a yearly ritual for those who live in cold country. Weather reports normally give you ample warning, so there is plenty of time to prepare. If you live in an area where heavy snows are probable, it's wise to stay prepared in case you are hit by that rare unforecasted storm.

The basic rules at the beginning of this chapter don't really apply to blizzards.

Before the blizzard:

- Fill your car's gas tank.
- Make sure you have tire chains or snow tires.
- Lay in a supply of wood for the fireplace.
- Have a supply of food that doesn't require heating or refrigerating (canned meats, bread, fruit).
- Check the batteries in your radio and flashlight.
- Have a supply of candles and matches.
- Get the extra blankets out of the attic, basement, or garage, and have them available.
- Have snow-removal gear on the porch, the carport, or garage.
- Store some water.

During the blizzard:

- Stay home. This is no time to walk or drive.
- You could be in for a siege lasting a few days. Have games to play and projects to work on.
- If your electricity goes off, consider putting refrigerator and freezer items out in the snow.
- In a car, try to find shelter immediately. Any school, restau-

rant, home, store, or office building will offer hospitality. If you get stuck on the road in a blizzard, get out just long enough to make sure your exhaust pipe is not plugged with snow, then get in and stay in. Crack one window about a half inch for ventilation. Run your engine about five minutes each half hour. If it's snowing hard, check the exhaust pipe each time before you start the engine. Don't leave the car running. You can't smell carbon monoxide, but it can kill you. Conserve your energy, but flex your joints and muscles enough to avoid cramping. If you run out of fuel, turn your dome light on. Surprisingly, this little light will generate some heat, especially if you remove its plastic shield.

If you live in an area where blizzards can be expected, you might consider keeping a few items in the car: a blanket, pair of warm gloves, scarf, pullover hat, crackers, a half-full plastic bottle of water (a full one would burst the bottle if it froze), and some type of energy food. Matches and candles could round out your "always in the trunk" emergency kit.

- If you are on foot, head for shelter immediately. Any building will do. If you can't find a building, try to get out of the wind in the lee of a hill or large tree. Snow has a certain amount of insulating quality. As a last resort, burrow in next to a tree, making sure to leave a breathing hole. Remember to continue flexing your muscles and get as much exercise as possible in the confined area.

After the blizzard, don't be in too big a rush to dig out. It may be some time until the streets are cleared, and shoveling snow is hard work! The wetter the snow, the heavier it will be. If your roof is flat or close to flat, lighten the load by removing some of the snow. Take it slow and easy.

Fire

Most fires strike with very little warning. They seem to hit most often in the middle of the night, when conditions for panic are greatest. Don't. Many survivors of serious fires will tell you that what got them through was their ability to push down panic, and to *think* about how to stay alive. Here are some basics:

- Plan ahead for the possibility of a house or apartment fire, providing at least two escape routes. Have everyone agree on a place to meet and count noses. Make sure that you and everyone who lives with you knows the routes and *stays* in the prearranged meeting place until all of you are sure everyone is safe.

- Every home and apartment should have a fire extinguisher. Make sure yours is a UL approved ABC type, so it will work on any type of fire.
- If the fire is too large for an extinguisher, get out of your house or apartment as quickly as possible. Call the fire department from a neighbor's phone.
- If you are trapped, open a window and stay near the floor. Keep a wet cloth over your face to breathe through.
- Don't open a door without first feeling it. If it is hot, don't open it. Try another.
- If you must open a door, crack it slowly. If you feel a rush of heat, slam it shut again.
- If you must exit through smoke-filled areas, keep low, breathe short breaths through your nose, and cover your face with a wet cloth. It takes only *three* breaths of black smoke to suffocate.
- Never go back into a burning building.
- In the event of a small electrical fire, have someone pull the main switch to shut off electricity. If an appliance is burning, pull the plug out of its socket. An electrical fire can be put out with a carbon dioxide or dry-chemical extinguisher. Baking soda is effective. *Never* use water to put out an electrical fire. It conducts electricity.
- Grease or oil fires must be smothered. *Never* put water on a grease or oil fire; it will only spread. Sand, baking soda, and carbon-dioxide or dry chemical extinguishers are best. If the fire is in a pan, simply cover and smother it.
- Small paper, cloth, or wood fires can be put out with water or with any of the materials just discussed.
- If your clothing should catch fire, fold your arms and roll on the floor. If possible, wrap a curtain, drape, or rug around you as you roll.
- If someone else's clothes are afire, wrap the victim in a sheet, blanket, drape, or whatever is handy, and roll him or her on the floor or ground. Don't try to undress anyone after the fire's out. You could further injure tender skin.

Precautions after a Disaster

After any disaster, some precautions should be taken. They are:

- Be alert and cautious.
- Before you turn your utilities back on: check for broken electrical lines; check for broken gas lines; check for broken water lines; report any problems to the utility companies.
- Don't light matches or fires until you are certain there are no gas leaks. Leaking gas plus fire will cause a violent explosion.
- Purify your water by boiling it for eight to ten minutes. If you can't boil the water, add one drop of chlorine bleach per quart of clear water, or three drops of bleach per quart of cloudy water, and let it stand for at least thirty minutes. The kind of bleach you use is important. Only bleach that has a label stating that it's *only* active ingrediant is hypochlorite may be safely used. If such chlorine is not available, you may substitute three drops per quart of a two percent solution of tincture of iodine for clear water. Double this amount if the water is cloudy.

MEDICAL EMERGENCIES

A woman in a restaurant suddenly gets up from the table, staggers a few steps, then falls writhing on the floor. Within minutes she is dead. The autopsy reveals that a piece of steak was caught in her windpipe.

A man leaves the elevator in his office building, clutches his heart, grimaces, and slumps to the floor. He is dead when the ambulance arrives, a victim of heart attack.

A small boy darts playfully after a ball on a downtown sidewalk, slips, and crashes through the display window of a store. He bleeds to death from a severed artery in his arm before professional help can arrive.

Every year, thousands of people die needlessly because no one standing by knows basic first aid. When you're faced with life-threatening emergencies, such as severe choking, heart failure, severe bleeding, or shock, prompt action can save a life. This section outlines types of emergencies and ways of dealing with each. They are *not* substitutes for professional help. These procedures *can,* however, be the difference between life and death for a victim.

After you've read this section, I urge you to take the basic first-aid course offered by your local Red Cross, and to call your community hospital to find out where to learn cardiopulmonary resuscitation (CPR) and how to help someone who is choking. The courses will reinforce what you learn here, and will stay with you all your life.

Basic Rules

- Do not move a victim unless it's absolutely necessary.
- Ask someone to get professional help.
- Don't panic. A life may depend on your calmness.

Severe Choking

The victim will usually try to dislodge whatever is stuck in his throat by coughing. As long as he or she is able to do this, you shouldn't attempt to help. If, however, he or she:

- gasps for breath
- has really violent fits of coughing
- turns pale and then blue, or cannot talk or breathe

you should quickly step to his aid. Proper treatment for choking is the following:

- Stand behind the choking victim with your arms around the victim just above the navel and below the rib cage.
- Lean the victim forward at the waist with his or her head and arms hanging down.
- Grasp your own fist, then exert pressure with a quick upward thrust against the victim's abdomen just above the navel to force air out of the lungs and expel the obstruction.
- Repeat this procedure until it is successful.
- After rescue, advise the victim to see a physician.

Mouth-to-Mouth Resuscitation

Breathing can be stopped as a result of suffocation, drowning, electrical shock, and other traumas. If you cannot feel air being

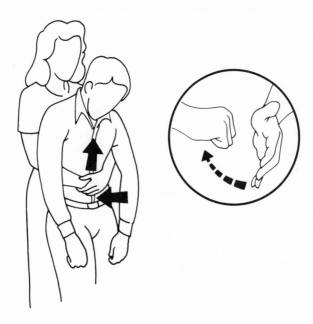

A sudden upward thrust just below the rib cage will expel a foreign object from a choking victim's windpipe.

expelled from the nose or mouth, or if the chest or abdomen does not rise and fall, begin treatment *immediately*.

- Position the victim on his back. If you must roll the victim over, try to roll him or her over in a single movement, keeping the back and neck straight. This helps prevent aggravation of any possible spinal injury.
- Quickly glance in victim's mouth for any obstruction (for example, food, tobacco, blood, dentures). If an obvious obstruction is present, carefully turn the victim on one side, tilt the head, and sweep the mouth out with your fingers. When the mouth is clear move the victim onto his back again and tilt the head back.
- Kneeling at the victim's side, tilt victim's head back so the chin points up by placing one hand under the neck and the other hand on the forehead.
- Check for breathing by bending over the victim, and placing

Make sure there are no obstructions in the victim's mouth.
Check for breathing. Then pinch the victim's nose closed and
breathe into his or her mouth.

your ear close to the mouth and nose. For at least five seconds
listen and feel for air exchange and look for chest movements.
- If the victim is not breathing, pinch the nose closed with the
hand that is resting on the forehead, form an airtight seal by
placing your mouth over the victim's mouth, and breathe into
the victim's mouth until his chest rises. If using the mouth-to-
nose method, seal the victim's mouth with your hand and
breathe in through his nose.
- Breathe into the patient a total of four times as quickly as possible. If you feel or hear no air exchange, tilt his head again
and try once more. If you still feel no air exchange, again
sweep the mouth of foreign objects, and breathe into the victim. If you still have no air exchange, turn the victim on his or
her side and slap the back between the shoulder blades. Again
sweep the mouth to remove foreign matter. Repeat if necessary.
- Repeat breathing. Remove your mouth each time to allow air
to escape. Repeat twelve times per minute for an adult, twenty
times per minute for a small child or infant. Use deep breaths
for adults, short puffs for children, and gentle puffs of your
cheeks for infants. As the victim begins to breathe, keep the
head tilted.

Circulatory Failure

Any time a victim is not breathing, check his or her pulse. If
you detect no heartbeat, there is an excellent technique to use.
But remember, *before using this technique,* you should have received training in cardiopulmonary resuscitation (CPR) from
your local hospital or Red Cross.

- Check the airway: Open the airway by tilting the victim's head back. (Victim should be on his or her back.)
- Check breathing: For at least five seconds listen and feel for air exchange and look for chest movements.
- If victim is not breathing: Give four quick full breaths, using the mouth-to-mouth resuscitation technique with the victim's nose pinched shut.
- Check pulse: After giving four quick breaths, check the pulse in the carotid artery in the neck. To find the carotid artery, locate the voice box and the large neck muscle. Press firmly but gently to feel for the pulse and hold for at least five seconds. If a pulse is not present, begin cardiac compressions immediately.
- Cardiac compressions: Kneel at the victim's side near his chest. The victim should be on a hard, flat surface. To determine the pressure point for cardiac compressions, locate the bony tip of the breastbone (sternum) with your ring finger and place your middle and index fingers just above that point. Your index finger will then be on the pressure point. Place the heel of the other hand next to your index finger. Now remove your fingers and place that hand on top of the other. Position your shoulders directly over victim's breastbone and press downward, keeping your arms straight. Depress an adult's sternum 1 ½ to 2 inches. Depress and release the sternum at regular intervals.

If you are the only rescuer, compressions should be at a rate of 80 per minute with two breaths (artificial ventilation) after each 15 compressions. Remember, after the two breaths,

Check the carotid artery for a pulse. Then locate the bony tip of the breastbone before applying cardiac compressions.

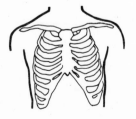
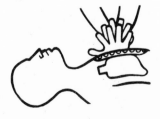

check your hand position on the sternum before resuming compressions.

If someone is helping you, each of you should be on opposite sides of the victim. One rescuer should perform compressions at a rate of about 60 per minute, while the second person interposes a breath (artificial ventilation) after every fifth compression. Compressions should not be interrupted when artificial respiration is being applied.

• Cardiopulmonary resuscitation for infants and small children:

1. Airway: Be careful not to overextend the infant's head when tilting it back; it is so pliable that you may block the breathing passage instead of opening it.
2. Breathing: Cover both mouth and nose with your mouth and release less air. Give a breath every three seconds.
3. Circulation: In both infants and small children only one hand is used for compressions. For infants, use only the *tips* of the index and middle fingers to depress the midsternum 1/2 to 3/4 inch at a rate of 80 to 100 compressions per minute. For small children, use only the heel of the hand to depress the chest at midsternum and depress the midsternum 3/4 to 1 1/2 inches, depending on the size of the child. The rates should be 80 to 100 compressions per minute.
4. In both small children and infants, breaths should be interposed after every fifth chest compression.

Severe Bleeding

The signs of severe bleeding are: the artery spurts bright-red blood; the vein continuously flows dark-red blood; with a capillary, blood oozes from the wound. Here's proper first aid treatment:

Apply direct pressure on the wound.

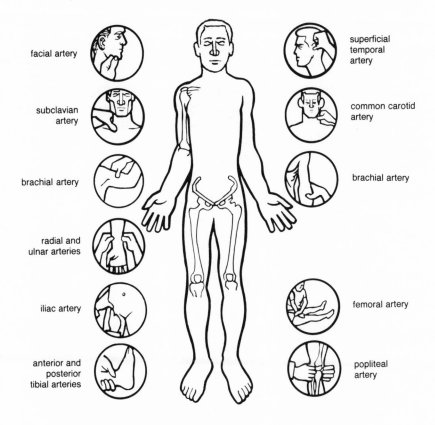

facial artery		superficial temporal artery
subclavian artery		common carotid artery
brachial artery		brachial artery
radial and ulnar arteries		
iliac artery		femoral artery
anterior and posterior tibial arteries		popliteal artery

These are the pressure points.

- Cover wound with the cleanest cloth immediately available or your bare hand. Apply *direct pressure* on the wound. Most bleeding can be stopped this way.
- Elevate the arm or leg as you apply pressure if there is no broken bone.
- Digital pressure at a pressure point controls bleeding from an arterial wound (bright-red blood spurting from it). Apply your fingers to the appropriate pressure point—a point where the main artery supplying blood to the wound is located (see diagram on this page). Hold the pressure point tightly for about five minutes or until the bleeding stops. The three pressure points in the head and neck should be used only as a last resort if, as in a skull fracture, direct pressure can't be used. If

direct pressure can be used, it will stop bleeding on the head in about 95 percent of the injuries.

Shock

Shock may accompany *any* serious injury: blood loss, breathing impairment, heart failure, burns, and many others. Shock can kill. Treat it as soon as possible and continue until medical aid is available.

The signs or symptoms of shock are:

• Shallow breathing.
• Rapid and weak pulse.
• Nausea, collapse, vomiting.
• Shivering.
• Pale, moist skin.
• Mental confusion.
• Drooping eyelids, dilated pupils.

The proper treatment for shock is:

• Establish and maintain an open airway.
• Control bleeding.
• Keep victim lying down. Exception: head and chest injuries, heart attack, stroke, sunstroke. If there is no spine injury, the victim may be more comfortable and breathe better in a semi-reclining position. If in doubt, keep the victim flat.
• Elevate the feet unless injury would be aggravated by this position.
• Maintain normal body temperature. Place blankets under and over victim.
• Give nothing by mouth, especially stimulants or alcoholic beverages.
• Always treat for shock in all serious injuries and watch for it in minor injuries.

Burns

There are first-, second-, and third-degree burns.

• First-degree burns cause reddened skin. To treat, immerse quickly in cold water or apply ice wrapped in a moist cloth until the pain stops.

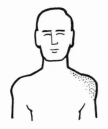 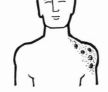 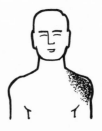

First degree burn   Second degree burn   Third degree burn

- Second-degree burns cause reddened skin and blisters. To treat, cut away loose clothing, cover with several layers of cold, moist dressing. If the limb is burned, immerse in cold water. Treat for shock.
- Third-degree burns destroy and damage and char tissues. To treat, cut away loose clothing (do not remove clothing adhering to skin), and cover with several layers of sterile, cold, moist dressings to relieve pain and stop burning action. Treat for shock.

11 | Consumer and Legal Aids

"Let the buyer beware" is as true today as it has been for ages, but one big difference helps to take the sting out of it. That difference is that many groups, organizations, and agencies are dedicated to helping you, the consumer, get what you paid for, and get it in a usable, safe condition.

This chapter will help you get the help you need when you have a small or large consumer problem.

CONSUMER TIPS

A ten-year-old boy was a guest recently on one of the network talk shows. His claim to fame was that he had learned how to complain—and get results! His technique was simplicity itself. For example, he had bought a construction set that had pieces missing. The store wouldn't listen to him. He was told he must have lost the pieces. The lad called the company, using the address on the box, collect, and asked for the president. The president accepted the call, listened to the boy, and sent him a new set!

Many of us are reluctant to complain when we should. We "don't want to make trouble," or we get no satisfaction when we do complain. All of us could learn something from the ten year old; complaints get results if we know how to go about making them.

No matter how careful you are in your purchases, sooner or later you'll get a bad deal or shoddy merchandise. It's a good idea to keep all of your receipts, contracts, warranties, and canceled checks in the same place. If a salesperson promises to repair or to deliver an item, it should be put in writing, too, and kept with all your other records.

Successful Complaining

The first rule of successful complaining is to speak out! If you keep your problem a secret, it will never be resolved. Here is a general procedure to follow when you have a complaint.

- Collect and organize records that pertain to the problem.
- Decide what you want the other party (store or business) to do. If you know what you want done and it's reasonable (don't insist on replacement of an item if it can be easily repaired, for example), you may get satisfaction from the first person you go to.
- Telephone or go in person. If you go in person, take your records with you.
- Explain the problem to the sales clerk. Be polite but firm. Explain what is wrong and what you think should be done about it.
- If the clerk can't help you, ask to speak to the manager or owner. The higher up you go, the better your chances of satisfaction. Go to the president of the organization if necessary!
- Be sure to let the store or business know that you will ask for outside help (Consumer Protection Agency, Action Line, or others) if you don't get satisfaction.

Recently, I bought a tour package to San Francisco from a local travel agency. The tour was short. It would begin early in the afternoon and include supper, and a special showing of the King Tut exhibition. I would return on the midnight flight. The day before departure, the agency called and apologetically explained that I'd been bumped from the return flight and would have to return early, thereby missing part of the King Tut showing, or stay overnight, at my own expense, or cancel the whole tour, to my disappointment. This seemed unfair to me. I'd paid my money and been told the reservation was confirmed. I didn't like any of the options, so I asked to speak to the manager of the agency. He wasn't available, of course, so I told them I would call the Consumer Protection Agency to ask for assistance. Two minutes after I hung up, the travel-agency manager called me.

Lo and behold! The problem had magically disappeared, "Just this very moment, Mrs. Hoyt." Obviously, he didn't want the Consumer Protection Agency in the act!

Higher Level Complaining

When the preceding course doesn't help, it's time to enlist extra assistance.

- Letters: To learn the name of the president of a large company, ask your librarian for the proper reference. Libraries have a number of reference books that contain this information. Then write, stating the name and serial number of the unsatisfactory product, and when and where you purchased it. Mention what you have already done to attempt to get satisfaction, and state the action you would like the people who get your letter to take. Enclose copies (not originals) of all the pertinent records. You might close with the statement that you will allow two weeks for resolution of your complaint before referring it to the appropriate consumer protection agency.

- Consumer Protection Agency: If all your other efforts have failed, contact your local Consumer Protection Agency, and it will refer you to the government agency that can help you. If you have no local agency, contact your state Consumer Protection Agency. It probably has a toll-free number. Consumer Protection Agencies act as clearing houses for many complaints, mediating those they are equipped to handle, and referring the others to the appropriate agencies.

  A book put out by the United States Government lists all the consumer offices in the country. It's name is, *Directory: Federal, State and Local Government Consumer Offices.* Your library should have it or you can send $2.00 for a copy to:

  Government Printing Office
  Washington, D.C. 20402

- State attorney general or local district attorney: Most states have a consumer fraud unit as part of the attorney general's office. If you have been the victim of an unfair business practice, write your attorney general in care of your state capitol. The attorney general does not handle your problem, but if his office receives enough evidence that a business is engaged in unfair practices, the attorney general can fine the business or order it to stop the practice. Your county district attorney can also help you if it is a local problem.

- Better Business Bureau: The Better Business Bureau is a nonprofit organization of private businesses. It can sometimes help arbitrate a dispute. This means that you try to negotiate a solution with the business you are having the problem with and a neutral third party. The BBB has some influence, but no actual authority. It cannot *make* the business go to arbitration, and cannot make it resolve the problem if the organization is not interested in a solution.
- Consumer Product Safety Commission: If you feel that a product is unsafe, write to the manufacturer and call the Consumer Product Safety Commission's hot line in Washington (1-800-638-2666).
- Federal Trade Commission: This agency regulates unfair business practices. It handles credit problems, misleading advertising, wrong labeling on clothing and household products, tricky business practices, warranty violations, and similar practices.

    The FTC does not handle individual problems, but when you file a complaint, the FTC will notify the business of your complaint. If a pattern of complaints from many consumers develops, it has the power to stop the unfair business practices.
- Legislators: If you have a complaint about a state or federal agency or consumer problems, your legislator might get results that you wouldn't be able to get on your own. To find out the name and address of your state or federal representative, call your local library.
- Action lines: Some newspaper and television stations help consumers settle their problems. The threat of bad publicity on TV or in the newspaper usually makes the business eager to settle the dispute. The media cannot handle all of the complaints they receive, but one of the many agencies and organizations listed here will be willing and able to help.

For Special Help

- Information and Referral, or Call for Action: These organizations can help you with your immediate problems or refer you to the right agency. They handle everything from consumer problems to personal problems, and are usually very kind and understanding.

Information and Referrals, or Call for Action, centers are staffed by both trained volunteers and salaried employees who can handle any situation: landlord problems, unemployment, hunger, suicide, and many others. If these organizations have offices in your city, call them when you or a friend has any kind of problem. There are seven hundred Information and Referral Services throughout the United States and they can be found in the white pages under "Information and Referral." "Call for Action" can be found in the following metropolitan areas:

WAKR	Akron, Ohio	WBSM	New Bedford, Mass.
WROW	Albany, N.Y.	WELI	New Haven, Conn.
KOB	Albuquerque, N.Mex.	WMCA	New York, N.Y.
WFBG	Altoona, Penn.	KWTV	Oklahoma City, Okla.
WGST	Atlanta, Ga.	WOW/KEZO	Omaha, Neb.
WBAL	Baltimore, Md.	WDBO	Orlando, Fla.
WYDE	Birmingham, Ala.	WRAU-TV	Peoria, Ill.
WBZ	Boston, Mass.	WFIL	Philadelphia, Penn.
WIVB-TV	Buffalo, N.Y.	KTAR-TV	Phoenix, Ariz.
WIND	Chicago, Ill.	KDKA	Pittsburgh, Penn.
WERE	Cleveland, Ohio	WJAR	Providence, R.I.
WDZ	Decatur, Ill.	WRAL-TV	Raleigh/Durham, N.C.
KLZ	Denver, Col.	CJRN	St. Catherines, Canada
WJR	Detroit, Mich.	KMOX	St. Louis, Mo.
WOWO	Ft. Wayne, Ind.	KGTV	San Diego, Ca.
WBAP	Ft. Worth, Tex.	WNEP-TV	Scranton, Penn.
WTLV-TV	Jacksonville, Fla.	WGSM	Suffolk County, N.Y.
KCMO	Kansas City, Kan.	WHEN	Syracuse, N.Y.
KARK-TV	Little Rock, Ark.	KTKT	Tucson, Ariz.
KFWB	Los Angeles, Ca.	WTLB	Utica, N.Y.
WDIA	Memphis, Tenn.	WTOP	Washington, D.C.
WCIX-TV	Miami, Fla.	WWVA	Wheeling, W.Va.
CFCF	Montreal, Canada	WFMJ	Youngstown, Ohio

The national headquarters are located at:

Call for Action
515 Lexington Avenue
New York, N.Y. 10022
1-212-355-5965

SMALL CLAIMS COURTS

Many of the problems we run into can be solved by using common sense. The situations that seem to be most frustrating are those in which someone has cheated us, owes us money and says he doesn't, backs out of an agreement to buy something from us, or sells something to us—in other words, a situation that's unfair, costs us money, and stymies our efforts to solve it. Of course we can sue, but lawyers are expensive and law suits seem to drag out forever.

It has been said that no cause is hopeless if it is just. The man who said it may have known of a relatively quick and inexpensive way to secure justice. You, too, will know of one by the time you've finished this section.

If you have a dispute and you are not getting any satisfaction, you will probably be able to find a simple, inexpensive way to solve your case in a Small Claims Court. These courts were set up to help those who need to recover relatively small amounts of money and could not afford lawyer's fees. The amount of money you can recover in small claims court varies from state to state, but runs from small amounts to a maximum range of $300 to $1,500. Those of us who are reluctant to sue because of high legal fees find the answer in these small claims courts. It's not necessary to have a lawyer (some states actually forbid them) and the procedure is relatively inexpensive and quick.

Finding the Small Claims Court

Small claims cases are tried in different courts, depending on the city or county government. In many states, small claims cases are tried by the local justices of the peace. You'll find "Justice of Peace" listed in the Yellow Pages of the telephone book. If these courts do not handle small claims, they can probably direct you to the right place. If not, call the city or county court or the Consumer Protection Agency and ask where your local Small Claims Court is located.

Getting Your Case on the Calendar

When you've located the small claims court, talk to the clerk of the court or the court clerk. This can be done in person or on the telephone. Briefly describe your problem. The clerk will be able to tell you if the Small Claims Court can handle it. Then you must go to the court, where the clerk will help you fill out the proper form. The clerk will answer your questions, take your completed form and fee, and schedule your case, normally within a month of your first visit. By the way, this would be a good time to audit one of the cases being heard in court to get an idea of what goes on and how things are done. Then, when your day comes, you'll feel more comfortable with the surroundings and the procedures.

At this point, the person your dispute is with won't have any idea (unless you've told him) that he has a date in court. The court clerk will draw up an order to be "served" on the person or firm you are suing. You pay another fee to have the court clerk hire someone to "serve" the order. The order tells the person you are suing (the *defendant*) that he or she is being sued and must appear at the stated time if he or she wishes to present a defense. The order must be served at least five days prior to the court date if the defendant lives or works in the same county, and fifteen days in advance if he lives and works elsewhere. Many of these cases never actually get to court because when the order is served the defendant pays to avoid the suit.

Preparing Your Case

While you wait for your trial date, gather all the papers you consider to be important evidence that you (the *plaintiff*) are right and have been done an injustice. These could be sales slips, sales contracts, bills, canceled checks, or warranties. Use this time to line up friendly witnesses. If they are willing to testify, make sure they know when and where to appear. Sometimes someone you wish to call as a witness is unwilling to be one. He may be a friend of the defendant and may not want his story to damage his friend. If his testimony is necessary, you can force him to appear through the "subpoena" process. The court clerk will advise you on how to have one issued. You should know, however, that this process is relatively more expensive, since an additional order must be written and served.

Your Day in Court

On the day of the trial, you and your witnesses should arrive early and check in with the court clerk, who will tell you which courtroom you'll be in. If an emergency comes up and you or your key witness can't be there, someone else can go at the appointed time to ask for a continuance. Make every effort, however, to be there for your court date. You'll have a few moments to arrange your evidence in the proper sequence before the judge or justice enters. When he does, all will rise and the clerk will announce your case. You, the plaintiff, and your witnesses will go forward and take the oath together, swearing that what you are about to say is the truth, the whole truth, and nothing but the truth. The others sit down. It is your turn to tell your story, present your evidence, and call your witnesses. Your testimony should be brief and to the point. The judge may ask questions, examine your papers, and talk to you to clarify any questions he or she has. Guard against the impulse to play Perry Mason. Be straightforward and open. *Don't* interrupt the judge, the witnesses, or the defendant!

When you're finished, the court hears the defendant's side of the story, complete with the evidence and witnesses the defendant has chosen to bring. After both sides of the case have been heard, the judge will render a decision—normally right there and then—but sometimes by mail a few days later if the judge wants to study the evidence presented. He or she may decide in your favor or in the defendant's favor, based upon the law and the facts presented. Presuming the judge decides in your favor, he or she will direct the defendant to pay you an amount that he considers just, which may or may not be the amount you have asked for. The procedure for this is that the judge instructs the clerk to "enter a judgment" against the defendant, who is then obligated to make payment to you. Remember, though, that the court is *not* a collection agent. It's up to you to get the money, but if the defendant refuses to pay or stalls, you can go back to the court clerk. The clerk will then write a "writ of execution," which instructs the sheriff to take something of value from the defendant to settle the debt.

If You're Being Sued

Chances are you'll never be a defendant in a small-claims action, but if you are, don't worry. If the claim is unfair, you'll have an opportunity to explain it to the judge. If it's a question of not being able to meet payments, you can ask, and probably receive, a new and lower payment schedule. Of course, if the claim *is* justified, you may be wise to settle it rather than go to court.

LAWYERS

Types of Lawyers

Lawyers, like doctors, are divided into two groups: general practitioners, who handle a variety of legal problems, and specialists, who handle only certain types of cases. Each state has its own requirements for general lawyers and specialists. Try to find a lawyer who spends a good deal of time practicing law in the area in which you have problems. To give you an idea of the different types of lawyers, I'll list some of the areas of specialization:

- Criminal law (felonies and juvenile law)
- Constitutional law (civil rights violations)
- Workmen's compensation (unemployment insurance, social security, and welfare)
- Family law (divorce, adoptions)
- Probate, wills, inheritance
- Bankruptcy
- Corporate law
- Personal injury

How to Find a Lawyer

Finding the right lawyer for your needs has become easier since the Supreme Court ruled that lawyers could advertise.

- Legal clinics have opened to handle routine problems—such as divorce, real estate, and consumer problems—at a fixed low fee. The clinics can be found in the Yellow Pages of the telephone book under "Lawyer," in newspaper advertisements, and even on television commercials.
- Friends or business people who have had similar problems can suggest a lawyer who was helpful to them.
- The Lawyer's Referral Service can provide a list of lawyers who are willing to accept new clients. For a small fee, they arrange a meeting and discussion between you and a lawyer on their list. You are under no obligation to use the lawyer. If you decide he or she is the right lawyer for you, you and the lawyer will agree on a fee and on the need for any future meeting.

Many new and inexperienced lawyers use the Lawyer's Referral Service as a way to get clients, and there's nothing wrong with that. Some services won't place lawyers on their referral list unless they have a certain amount of experience. All services will tell you their minimum requirements for lawyers. Ask about the lawyer's experience in the field in which you need help.

- A national directory of lawyers called *Martindale–Hubbell* can be found in your local library. This directory will give you additional information about the lawyer you're thinking of using. Only more experienced lawyers are included in *Martindale–Hubbell*.

Questions to Ask

The following are questions to ask an attorney when you're trying to pick the right one, according to the California Department of Consumer Affairs:

- What is the price range (high and low) for my type of case?
- Do you have a consultation fee? How much is it?
- What proportion of your practice is devoted to problems like mine? Ten percent? Half? Or more?
- Will you keep me informed of the progress of my case?

Contact various attorneys until you are satisfied with the answers to those questions. If you must contact an attorney about whom you know nothing, ask if he or she handles your type of case and what the approximate cost will be.

If the attorney asks you to visit his office rather than discuss fees over the telephone, ask if there is a charge for the office visit if you decide not to hire him. Many attorneys do not charge for a visit until you have decided to hire them. During the visit, get the information you need to decide whether the lawyer you are talking to is the right lawyer for you. *Don't* ask the attorney for legal advice before you are prepared to pay for it.

Your Relationship with Your Attorney

An attorney-client relationship is based upon trust. If you dislike or distrust your attorney, find someone else. When you visit the attorney's office, have the facts of your matter well in mind. Bring all necessary documents, names, and addresses. If you need advice quickly, call your attorney, but remember that you probably will be billed for a telephone consultation. Before you leave the office, make sure the attorney understands that you expect to be informed of the progress of your case.

Legal Fees

Your attorney's fee arrangement will depend on the type of case you have.

- Flat fee: Most routine and easily handled cases will be covered by a fee that covers everything, which is agreed upon in advance.
- Hourly rate: If the amount of work the lawyer may have to do is difficult to estimate, he may bill you for the time he actually works on your case. You can expect the hourly rate to be between $25 and $125 per hour.
- Contingent fee: If you've been injured in an accident and sue the other driver, your lawyer may want a "contingent" fee. If you lose, it costs you nothing. If you win, he gets a percentage, usually a third, of the amount awarded to you.

If You Can't Afford a Lawyer

Most communities offer free legal aid to those who can't afford a private attorney.

- Legal-aid services handle civil (no crime involved) matters. You'll find them in your Yellow Pages under "Attorneys" or "Lawyers."
- Public defender services handle criminal cases for those who can't afford to pay for them. They are also listed in the Yellow Pages under "Attorneys" or "Lawyers."
- Public-interest law firms specialize in cases that involve a large number of people. If you believe you have been victimized by price-fixing or faulty-manufacturing practices, a public-interest law firm will want to hear your story. There is no fee.

Complaints Against Attorneys

When a lawyer is admitted to the bar (allowed by the state to practice law), he or she is required to take an oath to obey the rules of ethics of the legal profession. If the lawyer fails to do so or fails to comply with the law, he or she is subject to disciplinary action by the state Bar Association.

If you have a disagreement with your attorney, try to work it out with him. Often this will result in an end to the disagreement. If it doesn't and you believe your lawyer is engaging in an unethical or illegal practice, report it to your state Bar Association. You'll find it listed under "Lawyers" or "Attorneys" in your Yellow Pages, or under the name of your state "Bar Association," in the white pages.

OTHER LEGAL INFORMATION

Here are a few other bits of information that may be useful.

Birth Certificates

To find out how to get your birth certificate, phone the Federal Information Center (white pages under "United States Government"). A clerk will tell you the address to write to, and the amount of money to send to receive your birth certificate from the state in which you were born. Give the following information.

- Full name, sex, race
- Your parents full names, including your mother's maiden name (mother's last name before she was married)
- Month, day, and year of your birth
- Place of birth
- Purpose for birth certificate

If you don't have all this information, send as much as you can.

Copyrights

If you've written a story, a song (lyrics or music, or both), or anything else you'd like to protect by copyright, Uncle Sam has devised a simple procedure. Here's how it works:

- Call the Federal Information Center (listed under "United States Government" in the white pages of your phone book).

- Explain what you want to copyright, and give the clerk your name and address.
- Fill in the forms they mail to you and enclose two copies of your material and a check or money order for $10. Mail them to:

> Library of Congress
> Copyright Office
> Crystal Mall
> 1921 Jefferson Davis Highway
> Arlington, Va. 20559

You don't need a lawyer for this service.

Not Responsible Signs

PARKING

> NOT RESPONSIBLE FOR DAMAGE, LOSS, OR THEFT!

HOTEL

> NOT RESPONSIBLE FOR VALUABLES LEFT IN YOUR ROOM!

GIFT STORE

> YOU PICK IT UP
> YOU BREAK IT
> YOU'VE BOUGHT IT
> PAY UP!

Signs like these are seen in many places, but they don't mean quite what they say.

- A parking lot *does* have some responsibility. No one is responsible for "acts of God," such as an earthquake or a flood, but

the parking lot has an obligation to take reasonable precautions to protect your car and its contents. The responsibility is greatest in lots that park the car for you, lock it, and keep your key.
- No sign or safe can relieve a hotel of all responsibility. It has a responsibility to safeguard your room and its contents. Most hotels and motels have a safe for extremely valuable items, and it's a good idea to use the service.
- The sign in the store does *not* make you liable for anything you may brush against and break. The store *is* responsible for displaying goods in such a way as to lessen opportunities for accidental damage. Deliberate damage, of course, is another story.

Why do businesses use signs like these? For two reasons: to attempt to limit their responsibility, and to try to make you believe that you alone are liable for whatever happens.

Only the circumstances of any incident determine who is liable and the extent of the liability, so *don't* believe the signs.

What If the Police Stop You?

Law-abiding citizens, as well as felons, are occasionally stopped and questioned by the police. When this happens, it's sometimes hard to remember that we (taxpayers) are the very ones who hire the police, pay their salaries, and instruct them to keep the law and order they're trying to maintain when they stop us.

The most important thing to do if you're stopped is to keep cool. Don't sound off. Don't resist arrest. And don't get mad. Don't resist arrest, even though you're innocent. That'll *really* get you into trouble!

You have certain rights, and the police have certain responsibilities. When both sides understand this, problems seldom occur.

If you're stopped for a minor traffic violation, the police can ask for your name, age, license, and registration. Since it is a minor incident, you should answer other questions without concern or antagonism.

If, however, you're stopped and asked about a crime that has been committed, ask to have a lawyer present before you give any information other than your name and age. The United

States Supreme Court has ruled that the police *must* inform you of your rights and risks before they can ask you questions as a part of a criminal investigation. Here are your rights:

- You have the right to remain silent.
- You have the right to have an attorney present. If you can't afford one, the court will appoint an attorney to represent you.
- You may refuse to answer questions at any point during an interrogation.

If the police arrest you, give your name, address, and telephone number. Don't answer *any* questions until your lawyer is present. The police can photograph and fingerprint you, and then you are allowed one phone call. Call a relative or friend, explain where you are and what you are being held for. You might also ask him or her to get a lawyer for you.

Voting

Election laws vary throughout the country, so you will have to check with your local Voter Registration Office or League of Women Voters to find out what the requirements are in your state. In general, every resident of a state is qualified to vote if he or she:

- Is a citizen of the United States.
- Will be eighteen years old or older prior to the next regular gubernatorial or presidential general election. (General elections are held in even-numbered years.)
- Will be a resident of the state for a certain number of days (usually thirty to fifty) before the next election.
- Is able to write his or her name or make his or her mark.
- Has not been convicted of treason or a felony.

Most states have several locations where you can register, including:

- County Registrar's Office.
- Political party headquarters (Republican, Democratic, Libertarian and so on).
- Deputy registrars, who live in all areas of the state; contact

them through your Voter's Registration Office or Department of Elections.

* Justices of the peace in some small towns.

If for some reason you will not be able to cast your vote at the polling place near your home, you may obtain an absentee ballot. Phone your local Department of Elections or County Recorder to find out when the absentee ballots will be issued. They are usually issued thirty to fifty days before the election. You may vote at the elections office or have the ballot and instructions mailed to you. If you have them mailed, your vote must be witnessed and signed by a notary public or deputy registrar. Usually, the absentee ballot must be in the office of the Department of Elections by closing time on election day.

12 | Government Services

In 1800, when President Adams moved into the White House, there were 6 federal agencies. Now there are more than 125 agencies and departments, with more than 4 million employees. It's a big bureaucracy, hard to find your way around in, but it is peopled by literally thousands of conscientious civil servants who are there to help *you.*

GETTING THE GOVERNMENT TO HELP SOLVE YOUR PROBLEM

Government agencies supply practically any information under the sun whenever you request it—and it's free, or available for a nominal cost. Do you want to know what office handles food stamps? Are you interested in learning how to buy surplus government property? Do you need information on income taxes? Passports? Joining the Navy? Ask your closest Federal Information Center!

The federal government is also the largest single employer in the world. In general, the pay scales are higher than those in industry or commerce. Benefits are also better. Job security is well above that of other sectors of the economy.

Your government exists to be of assistance to you, so in this chapter we'll take a tour of some specific areas of the government that can help.

The number of agencies, programs, and activities carried on

by the government is so vast that no one person knows where to go for help in all circumstances. Getting shunted from one government office to another, and another, and another can become so discouraging that you finally give up in despair.

Federal Information Centers

The government has set up Federal Information Centers (FICs) to avoid this very problem. These centers are staffed by specially trained people who are knowledgeable and helpful. They steer you to the proper program or agency to solve your particular problem. My own experience with the Phoenix Federal Information Center is that they have gone out of their way to help me find answers to any question I have asked them.

The centers often steer you toward problem-solving state and local agencies if those agencies can do a better or quicker job than the federal government.

No question is too simple or too complex for a Federal Information Center to handle. There are FICs in thirty-five states and the District of Columbia. A list of their phone numbers and addresses appears on page 154. Call or write to the one nearest you for assistance.

Legislators

We often think our senators and congresspeople are too busy with great affairs to care about our individual problems. The fact is, however, your legislators are willing to help. Most of them have "problem solvers" on their staffs, who are skilled at unsnarling the red tape that often seems to surround problems with unemployment benefits, welfare, and so on.

The names of your local, state, and federal representatives can be found by calling your local library, which has a reference department that will find this information for you.

If you have a problem or want to express your own opinion on any issue, write to:

Your Congressperson, Your State
c/o U.S. House of Representatives
Washington, D.C. 20510

You can also send a public-opinion telegram to let elected officials know your views on issues immediately. This is much cheaper than a regular telegram (see Chapter 13).

Federal Information Centers

Alabama

Birmingham
322-8591
Toll-free tieline to
Atlanta, Ga.

Mobile
438-1421
Toll-free tieline to
New Orleans, La.

Arizona

Phoenix
(602) 261-3313
Federal Building
230 North First Ave.
85025

Tucson
622-1511
Toll-free tieline to
Phoenix

Arkansas

Little Rock
378-6177
Toll-free tieline to
Memphis, Tenn.

California

Los Angeles
(213) 688-3800
Federal Building
300 North Los
Angeles St.
90012

Sacramento
(916) 440-3344
Federal Building and
U.S. Courthouse
650 Capitol Mall
95814

San Diego
(714) 293-6030
Federal Building
880 Front St.
Room 1S11
92188

San Francisco
(415) 556-6600
Federal Building and
U.S. Courthouse
450 Golden Gate Ave.
P.O. Box 36082
94102

San Jose
275-7422
Toll-free tieline to
San Francisco

Santa Ana
836-2386
Toll-free tieline to
Los Angeles

Colorado

Colorado Springs
471-9491
Toll-free tieline to
Denver

Denver
(303) 837-3602
Federal Building
1961 Stout St.
80294

Pueblo
544-9523
Toll-free tieline to
Denver

Connecticut

Hartford
527-2617
Toll-free tieline to
New York, N.Y.

New Haven
624-4720
Toll-free tieline to
New York, N.Y.

District of Columbia

Washington
(202) 755-8660
Seventh and
D Sts., S.W.
Room 5716
20407

Florida

Fort Lauderdale
522-8531
Toll-free tieline to
Miami

Jacksonville
354-4756
Toll-free tieline to
St. Petersburg

Miami
(305) 350-4155
Federal Building
51 Southwest
First Ave.
33130

Orlando
422-1800
Toll-free tieline to
St. Petersburg

St. Petersburg
(813) 893-3495
William C. Cramer
Federal Building
144 First Ave., South
33701

Tampa
229-7911
Toll-free tieline to
St. Petersburg

West Palm Beach
833-7566
Toll-free tieline to
Miami

Georgia

Atlanta
(404) 221-6891
Federal Building
275 Peachtree St., N.E.
30303

Hawaii

Honolulu
(808) 546-8620
Federal Building
300 Ala Moana Blvd.
P.O. Box 50091
96850

Illinois

Chicago
(312) 353-4242
Everett McKinley
Dirksen Building
219 South Dearborn St.
Room 250
60604

Indiana

Gary/Hammond
883-4110
Toll-free tieline to
Indianapolis

Indianapolis
(317) 269-7373
Federal Building
575 North
Pennsylvania
46204

Iowa

Des Moines
284-4448
Toll-free tieline to
Omaha, Nebr.

Kansas

Topeka
295-2866
Toll-free tieline to
Kansas City, Mo.

Wichita
263-6931
Toll-free tieline to
Kansas City, Mo.

Kentucky

Louisville
(502) 582-6261
Federal Building
600 Federal Place
40202

Louisiana

New Orleans
(504) 589-6696
U.S. Postal Service
Building
701 Loyola Ave.
Room 1210
70113

Maryland

Baltimore
(301) 962-4980
Federal Building
31 Hopkins Plaza
21201

Massachusetts

Boston
(617) 223-7121
J.F.K. Federal
Building
Cambridge St.
Lobby, 1st Floor
02203

Michigan

Detroit
(313) 226-7016
McNamara Federal
Building
477 Michigan Ave.
Room 103
48226

Grand Rapids
451-2628
Toll-free tieline to
Detroit

Minnesota

Minneapolis
(612) 725-2073
Federal Building and
U.S. Courthouse
110 South Fourth St.
55401

Missouri

Kansas City
(816) 374-2466
Federal Building
601 East Twelfth St.
64106

St. Joseph
233-8206
Toll-free tieline to
Kansas City

St. Louis
(314) 425-4106
Federal Building
1520 Market St.
63103

Nebraska
Omaha
(402) 221-3353
Federal Building
U.S. Post Office and
Courthouse
215 North 17th St.
68102

New Jersey
Newark
(201) 645-3600
Federal Building
970 Broad St.
07102

Paterson/Passaic
523-0717
Toll-free tieline to
Newark

Trenton
396-4400
Toll-free tieline to
Newark

New Mexico
Albuquerque
(505) 766-3091
Federal Building and
U.S. Courthouse
500 Gold Ave., S.W.
87102

Santa Fe
983-7743
Toll-free tieline to
Albuquerque

New York
Albany
463-4421
Toll-free tieline to
New York

Buffalo
(716) 846-4010
Federal Building
111 West Huron St.
14202

New York
(212) 264-4464
Federal Building
26 Federal Plaza
Room 1-114
10007

Rochester
546-5075
Toll-free tieline to
Buffalo

Syracuse
476-8545
Toll-free tieline to
Buffalo

North Carolina
Charlotte
376-3600
Toll-free tieline to
Atlanta, Ga.

Ohio
Akron
375-5638
Toll-free tieline to
Cleveland

Cincinnati
(513) 684-2801
Federal Building
550 Main St.
45202

Cleveland
(216) 522-4040
Federal Building
1240 East Ninth St.
Room 137
44199

Columbus
221-1014
Toll-free tieline to
Cincinnati

Dayton
223-7377
Toll-free tieline to
Cincinnati

Toledo
241-3223
Toll-free tieline to
Cleveland

Oklahoma
Oklahoma City
(405) 231-4868
U.S. Post Office and
Courthouse
201 Northwest 3rd St.
73102

Tulsa
584-4193
Toll-free tieline to
Oklahoma City

Oregon
Portland
(503) 221-2222
Federal Building
1220 Southwest
Third Ave.
Room 109
97204

Pennsylvania
Allentown/Bethlehem
821-7785
Toll-free tieline to
Philadelphia

Philadelphia
(215) 597-7042
Federal Building
600 Arch St.
Room 1232
19106

Pittsburgh
(412) 644-3456
Federal Building
1000 Liberty Ave.
15222

Scranton
346-7081
Toll-free tieline to
Philadelphia

Rhode Island
Providence
331-5565
Toll-free tieline to
Boston, Mass.

Tennessee
Chattanooga
265-8231
Toll-free tieline to
Memphis

Memphis
(901) 521-3285
Clifford Davis Federal
Building
167 North Main St.
38103

Nashville
242-5056
Toll-free tieline to
Memphis

Texas
Austin
472-5494
Toll-free tieline to
Houston

Dallas
749-2131
Toll-free tieline to
Fort Worth

Fort Worth
(817) 334-3624
Fritz Garland Lanham
Federal Building
819 Taylor St.
76102

Houston
(713) 226-5711
Federal Building and
U.S. Courthouse
515 Rusk Ave.
77002

San Antonio
224-4471
Toll-free tieline to
Houston

Utah
Ogden
399-1347
Toll-free tieline to
Salt Lake City

Salt Lake City
(801) 524-5353
Federal Building
125 South State St.
Room 1205
84138

Virginia
Newport News
244-0480
Toll-free tieline to
Norfolk

Norfolk
(804) 441-6723
Stanwick Building
3661 East Virginia
Beach Blvd.
Room 106
23502

Richmond
643-4928
Toll-free tieline to
Norfolk

Roanoke
982-8591
Toll-free tieline to
Norfolk

Washington
Seattle
(206) 442-0570
Federal Building
915 Second Ave.
98174

Tacoma
383-5230
Toll-free tieline to
Seattle

Wisconsin
Milwaukee
271-2273
Toll-free tieline to
Chicago, Ill.

National Suggestion Box

If you have an idea that you think the government could use, send it to:

National Suggestion Box
Box 2009
Washington, D.C. 20013

If they think they can use your idea, they will notify you.

Equal Employment Opportunity Commission (EEOC)

This commission guarantees equal opportunity for employment without regard to race, color, sex, religion, or national origin. If you feel that there has been discrimination against you, contact your nearest district office of EEOC or write:

Director, Office of Public Affairs
Equal Employment Opportunity Commission
Washington, D.C. 20506

Consumer-Protection Groups

The federal government protects broad masses of people from unfair consumer practices. As a matter of fact, the consumer agency of your state or local government may be a lot more helpful to you than will the federal government.

Here are some of the many federal consumer groups:

- The Office of Consumer Affairs advises the President on matters of consumer interest, coordinates all federal activities in the consumer field, seeks ways to aid and protect the consumer.
- The Bureau of Consumer Protection (Federal Trade Commission) has programs to alert the public to deceptive trade practices.
- The Consumer Product Safety Commission develops safety standards for consumer products in order to protect the consumer from unreasonable risks. To complain about the safety of any product, call toll free 1-800-638-2666 (in Maryland call 1-800-492-2937).

These groups get involved in the every-day consumer problems of the average citizen. The easiest way to find out which group is most likely to be able to help you is to call your Federal Information Center. It keeps lists of state and local consumer groups as well as the federal ones.

If you have an *immediate* problem of almost any kind, phone the closest Call for Action or Information and Referral center, near you.

Community Services

Each community offers some or all of the services listed below. To find out what services your community offers, call the information office at your city or town hall.

- Information and Referral services
- General services, including economic assistance, counseling, youth services, Red Cross, and so on
- Emergency services, such as suicide prevention, counseling for rape victims, aid for battered or neglected children, and help in similar crisis situations
- Mental health services, such as counseling services and mental health treatment centers
- Alcohol and drug-abuse services, including Alcoholics Anonymous, Alanon, Alateen, and similar groups
- Legal assistance services, such as Lawyer's Referral and the Legal Aid Society

GENERAL INFORMATION SERVICES

Government agencies are chock-full of interesting and helpful information. Here are some resources that may interest you.

Government Publications

The Consumer Information Center, located in Pueblo, Colorado, publishes hundreds of pamphlets with information for the consumer. The titles range from *The Backyard Mechanic* to *In Pursuit of a Summer Tan.* Most of the pamphlets are free. The others range from 10¢ to $1.25. To get a list of all the pamphlets write for *The Consumer Information Catalogue* to:
Consumer Information Center
Pueblo, Colo. 81009
Write "Catalogue" on the outside of your envelope to speed delivery.

Library of Congress

Books and other reference materials are available for use by the public in the library's sixteen reading rooms. When you cannot obtain a book at a local library, the local library may borrow the book from the Library of Congress through the inter-library service. This library has:

- Division for the Blind and Physically Handicapped: provides Braille and recorded books for those who cannot read.
- Copyright Office: registers personal creative works (such as books, music, see Chapter 11).
- National Referral Center for Science and Technology: directs you to organizations or individuals that can help you with your research (great for research papers).
- General Reference and Bibliography Division: answers written questions that can't be answered with local, state, and regional sources (great for research papers).

Other Public Libraries

Many chapters of this book have suggested that you look at various reference books available at your local library. Most libraries have a "reference librarian" who will be happy to get the book you want to see.

Some libraries also have a telephone service. The librarian looks up the information you want and reads it to you over the phone.

Libraries offer a host of services including records, tapes, and films. The following are a few of the services you should know about.

- Reserved books: If the book you want is not on the shelf, but listed in the card catalog, ask the librarian to put your name on the reservation list. When the book comes in, he or she will phone or send you a postcard telling you that the book is available and will be held in your name for a certain period of time. Some libraries charge a small fee for reservations.
- Interlibrary books: If your library doesn't have a copy of the book you want, it can usually obtain it for you from another library. There is a small fee for this service, but if you need the book, it's worth it.

- Subject reference books (bibliographies): A bibliography lists all the books printed under certain subject headings, such as Fine Arts, Mathematics, or Law, listing the name and author of each book written about a specific subject. Some of these books are called annotated bibliographies because they also briefly describe the contents of the books. They are more helpful than "title and author" listings.
- Reference books: Here are some other types of references that can be very useful when you're digging for information.
  1. *Books in Print* lists all the books and paperbacks published in a given year. It lists the books by subject, title, and author.
  2. *The Reader's Guide to Periodic Literature* lists all the articles published in magazines and journals for the year by subject and date of publication.
  3. *Reader's Advisor's Guide* is a good self-study reference book.
  4. *Sheehy's Guide to Reference Material* is great for school reports and research.
- Records, tapes, and films: Records and tapes are usually borrowed under the same system as books. Films are usually rented, however.

Freedom of Information Act

This act requires that all federal agencies must open most of their files to any person who writes for the information. You can even find out if the FBI or CIA has a file on you and what's in the file. Every government agency has a Freedom of Information division that handles any written request for information from that agency within ten days. There is a fee for the time spent locating the file or information you requested, so you should give an organized, detailed report with your request. There are only nine reasons that the government can use to withhold the information you seek, and these involve invasion of a person's privacy and classified government information.

Government Hot Lines

Some government agencies have set up hot lines so that you can call a central office toll-free for help and guidance. Here's the latest list released by Ralph Nader's Public Citizen's Group:

- Travel: 1-800-323-4180 (Illinois 1-800-942-4833). Answers questions about tourist attractions, transportation, and lodgings.
- Federal tax information: Call 1-800-555-1212. Ask for the number of the regional office closest to you. Answers questions on income tax problems.
- Venereal disease: 1-800-523-1885 (Pennsylvania 800-4966). Gives information and referral services to anonymous callers.
- Federal Crime Insurance: 1-800-638-8780 (Washington D.C. and Maryland 652-2637). How to apply for low-cost commercial or residential crime insurance.
- Educational grants: 1-800-638-6700, dispenses information about government subsidized higher education. Call 1-800-553-6350 for information and assistance in processing your application.
- National Runaway Hot Line: 1-800-621-4000 (Illinois 1-800-972-6004). Confidential twenty-four-hour-a-day advisory information to runaways and their parents. Also will call a parent at the request of a runaway (does not disclose the location of the runaway) to pass a message.
- Occupational Safety and Health Administration: 1-800-555-1212 for the nearest regional number. Accepts reports about hazardous working conditions.
- Consumer Product Safety Commission: 1-800-638-2666 (Maryland 1-800-492-2937). Helps callers evaluate the safety of products and takes reports on injuries or deaths related to them.
- Fair Housing and Equal Opportunity Hot Line: 1-800-424-8950 (Washington D.C. 755-5490). Takes complaints on race, religious, or sex discrimination.
- Interstate Commerce Commission: 1-800-424-9312 (Washington D.C. 275-7301). Takes complaints about train or bus passenger problems and about moving of household goods.
- National Highway Safety Administration: 1-800-424-9393 (Washington D.C. 426-0123). Answers questions about automobile recalls and accepts reports about auto-safety problems.

13 | Communications Services

Many people lead somewhat nomadic lives. We were counting the other day, and we realized that our son Mike has gone to twelve schools, Ed has gone to seven, Jim and John to five each. That's a lot of moves, and it points out that moving things—people, furniture, merchandise, messages, voices, pictures—is one of the most important tasks that industry faces today.

What's the cheapest way to send it? Why is my telephone bill so high? How can I be sure it got there safely? What if I need to get it there quickly? How can I prove that I really mailed it? These and other questions are answered in this chapter.

THE UNITED STATES POSTAL SERVICE

Pony express riders thundering across the prairies; Charles Lindbergh flying some of the first air mail; the mail going through despite wind, rain, and dark of night—the United States Postal Service has a romantic past, but the challenges it faces today are no less demanding.

The United States Postal Service routinely handles the largest volume of any post office in the world today. It's worth taking a close look at the services it offers.

- First-class mail is used for postcards and personal letters as well as most business letters. First-class mail insures privacy and cannot be opened for inspection. It is the most expensive of the three classes of mail but also the fastest, except for express mail.

- Second-class mail is usually used for newspapers and magazines. You may use it to mail individual copies.
- Advertisers use third class the most, but individuals mailing lightweight parcels can use it too. Ask your post office.
- Fourth class mail is a special book rate.
- Special delivery, according to the post office, provides for delivery outside routine delivery hours and on Sundays and holidays. There's an extra fee for this service. Experience shows that the additional handling usually slows the mail down. First-class mail often reaches its destination faster.
- Express mail guarantees overnight delivery for letters and parcels but is not available everywhere. Check with your local post office. Remember, *never* send cash through the mail. Express service is expensive, so be sure you really need it.

Proof of Mailing and Delivery

A few years ago, we bought a smokeless broiler through an advertisement that promised your money back within thirty days if you were not satisfied with the product. We weren't. It was shiny and efficient looking, and the quartered chicken burned with a beautiful yellow flame the first time we used it.

When we mailed the broiler back, we paid a small extra fee for a certified return receipt. Then, when the company denied ever having received it, we sent them a copy of the receipt, and our money was returned in the next mail.

A *return receipt* is proof of delivery. It is available for a fee on any insured, certified, or registered mail. You might ask at the post office for a return receipt, and after the item is delivered you will receive in the mail a receipt telling you the date it was delivered and who signed for it. For an additional fee, you can request that the letter be delivered to and signed for *only* by the person to whom the letter is addressed.

A *certificate of mailing* can be used if all you need is proof that you mailed the item, not when it was delivered. It does not provide insurance for loss or damage. It is a very inexpensive record of mailing.

Certified mail provides you with both a mailing receipt and a record of delivery at the post office nearest the receiver of the letter. If *you* want proof of delivery for the item, ask for a certified return receipt.

Sending Valuable Items through the Mail

Never send money (bills or coins) through the mail. Cash can be sent safely by your bank or by telegram. Many other valuable things, such as important documents, can be mailed, however. Here's how:

- Insured Mail is protected up to $200. The cost is determined by the amount of insurance you need. You can have a return receipt for an extra fee.
- Registered mail is used to send very valuable items and all items costing over $200. When you register an item to be mailed, you must declare its value (tell how much it's worth). Included in the fee for registered mail is insurance protection up to $10,000 for mail inside the United States. For an extra fee you can have a return receipt on registered mail.

Other Services

- Special handling is for parcels that require careful attention, such as fruits or breakable materials. Ask at the window for this extra service. It costs a little more but helps to get packages to their destination safely. Remember to purchase insurance if the parcel is valuable.
- If you're moving, forms available at the post office will direct all your mail to be forwarded to your new address for a period of time. First-class mail will be forwarded for a full year, but it is best to inform everyone you expect to receive mail from of your new address as quickly as possible. The post office will give you change-of-address forms for this purpose if you ask for them.
- If you're leaving for a short period and don't want mail to stack up in your box, there's a form at the post office that will direct postal clerks to hold your mail until you return from your trip.
- A large zip code directory that looks like a huge dictionary is kept in the front part of the post office. You may go in at any time and look up the zip code for any part of the country. If you can't go to the post office, call and tell them the address you need a zip code for and a post office clerk will look it up for you. Some cities have a special number for this purpose.

Mail Fraud, Junk Mail, and Mail Order Problems

- Mail fraud: The Postal Inspection Service protects the rights of people who may have been defrauded through the mails. This service will investigate and stop any fraud that is brought to its attention. If you have any reason to suspect that you are being victimized by a mail-fraud scheme, call the Postal Inspection Service immediately. It will even try to get your money back for you!
- Junk mail: To remove your name from any mailing list, call your local post office, and ask for the proper form to fill out.

  If you get lots of junk mail, there is an organization you can write to that will remove your name from its files. Write for a name-removal form to:

  > Direct Mail/Marketing Association
  > 6 East 43rd Street
  > New York, N.Y. 10017

- Mail order: Mail-order problems can be resolved with the help of the Postal Inspection Service. To avoid these problems in the first place, use the following checklist when ordering merchandise through the mail:

  1. Be sure you make out the order form clearly and completely.
  2. Keep a copy of the company's address for future reference.
  3. *Never send cash* in the mail! Be sure to include all the extra charges in your payment. COD orders cost you more.
  4. Upon delivery, check to make sure you've received what you wanted. If not, notify the company and return the item. Be sure to get some proof of mailing from the post office.

  If you do run into problems, you should know that federal law gives you certain rights:

  1. You have the right to know when an item you've ordered will be shipped (within thirty days is the legal time unless the mail-order house states otherwise in its advertisement).
  2. If the item is not shipped within the agreed time, you can cancel the order and get a full refund.
  3. It is illegal to send goods through the mail that have not been ordered. If you receive unordered merchandise, you may legally consider it a free gift!

Coin-Operated Substations

The post office maintains a large number of conveniently located, unattended, coin-operated substations. At these locations, you can purchase stamps through vending machines, weigh and determine postage for packages, and mail letters and packages. There's a telephone receiver at each of these substations, and a post office employee will answer your questions if you pick it up.

The stamp-vending machines occasionally accept your money and refuse to issue your stamps. Don't kick the machine. Pick up the telephone and report the problem. The post office will mail your stamps with its apologies immediately.

PARCELS AND PACKAGES

Parcels and packages are handled not only by the United States Post Office but also by a number of commercial enterprises. We'll look at a number of them:

United States Postal Service Parcel Post

This is the most widely used service for mailing packages that weigh more than a pound. There are different rates for different types of service. I have found that if I ask, "What is the *fastest* way to mail my package?" or if time is not important, "What is the *cheapest* way to mail my package?" I can get the service that suits my needs at the lowest cost. When you're in a special hurry, ask about the priority-mail system that allows your package to be handled in the same manner as first-class mail.

United Parcel Service

For packages, the shipping rates of United Parcel Service (UPS), a private company, are often lower than those of the post office. Delivery is often faster, as well. The best way to use UPS is to take your package to their office. They will, however, pick it up at your home or office for an extra fee. You'll find United Parcel Service in your phone book.

Major Bus Companies

Bus lines have excellent parcel services. Check your phone book and call for information.

Air Freight

Shipping parcels by air is expensive, but when time is important, you'll find air-freight companies fast and efficient. Look under "Air Freight Companies" in your Yellow Pages.

Preparing a Package for Mailing

Correct preparation for shipping is not hard and is your best insurance that the package will arrive in good condition. Here are some pointers:

- Use a carton that's strong enough to withstand a lot of bumping around.
- Insulate the contents with shredded paper, foam, or other packing material.
- Tape generously with a high-strength tape. The days of brown paper and string are over.
- Make sure that the address is clear and correct. Include your return address.

SENDING MONEY QUICKLY AND SAFELY

Occasionally you'll need to send or receive money in a hurry. You should know how to do it.

Money Orders

Chapter 5 explains postal money orders or cashiers' checks. You can mail these by express mail and be assured of quick delivery. Remember, *do not* send cash through the mail.

Bank-to-Bank Transfers

Many banks telegraph money from one city to another at your instruction. If you want to transfer money from your bank to someone else's account in another bank in another city, ask your bank if it has this service. It's normally free.

Western Union

We'll discuss the services offered by Western Union later in this chapter, but we'll tell you here about its money-transferring service.

If you must send money quickly, wire it through Western

Union. The recipient can pick it up from two to four hours after you send it. Simply take it to a Western Union office, and, for a fee determined by the amount of money you want to send, it will be wired. Give the telephone number of the person receiving the money. Once it reaches the other city, Western Union phones the person and he or she picks it up or Western Union will deliver it for an extra fee.

TELEPHONE TIPS

The Best Times to Call

The telephone company has different rates for the same call, depending on when and how you place it. You can save by dialing direct instead of asking an operator to help you. You save even more if you dial direct at the right time of day. Charges are determined as follows:

Rate	*Time*
Full rate	weekdays (Monday through Friday) 8 A.M. to 5 P.M.
35 percent discount	evenings (Sunday through Friday) 5 P.M. to 11 P.M.
60 percent discount	nights 11 PM. to 8 A.M., and 11 P.M. Friday to 5 P.M. Sunday

Holiday day rates are the same as evening rates.

To be sure you are getting the right rate, wait at least five minutes past the times given here (8 A.M., 5 P.M., 11 P.M.).

Take advantage of time zones. People on the west coast should call the east in the morning before 8 A.M. (11 A.M. on the east coast.) People in the east should call the west in the evening after 11 P.M. (8 P.M. on the west coast.)

Person-to-Person Calls

If you must speak to one specific person only, make an operator-assisted call and give the name of the person with whom you wish to speak. The operator will handle the call, and if the person you are calling is not there, you are not charged. This call is expensive if it is completed, but it's useful when you're not sure the person you want to talk to is available.

Emergency Calls

The telephone operator (dial 0) is trained and equipped to handle a wide variety of emergency situations. In addition to helping callers reach the fire and police departments, the operator can contact a list of many other emergency numbers, such as poison control, drug-abuse, and suicide prevention services. In an emergency situation, the operator will remain cool, try to pinpoint the required service, and do everything in his or her power to help.

Wrong Numbers and Bad Connections

If you accidently dial a long-distance number incorrectly or get a noisy connection, hang up and dial 0. The operator will put the call through for you at the dial-direct rate and will adjust your bill to remove the cost of the first call.

Toll-Free Numbers

A toll-free number is a phone number you can use without having to pay for it. This service is offered by many large companies and government offices. To find out whether an organization you want to call has a toll-free number, dial toll-free information, 1-800-555-1212, and ask the operator.

Telephone Book Information

The phone book can give you a great deal of information about the city you live in. Look through the front and back sections of the phone book and you will find maps of the city, zip-code information, and emergency numbers. The "Frequently Requested Numbers" under state and federal government listings are a real help. Check the phone book out, especially if you're new to a city.

WESTERN UNION TELEGRAPH SERVICES

Telegrams

A telegram is a message sent by wire. The message can reach anywhere in the United States in one-and-a-half to two hours. You can phone or visit your local Western Union office to send the message. Rates vary, but for a specified fee you can send up to fifteen words. There is an additional charge for extra words.

The message is wired to the city nearest the person to receive it and then relayed by phone to that person. Western Union then mails a copy of the telegram, or delivers it for an extra fee.

Night Letters

You can send a message up to one-hundred words for a certain fee (extra words cost more). The night letter is wired to the destination and then telephoned to the receiver between 9 A.M. and 2 P.M. the following day. For an extra fee, it will be delivered. A night letter is much cheaper than a telegram.

Mailgram

You can send a message of up to one-hundred words for a given fee (extra words cost more). The mailgram is wired to the destination and then put in the regular mail to be delivered by the postman. It is cheaper than a night letter.

Public Opinion Message

If you are sending a message to any elected federal, state, or local official, you can use a public opinion message. It is usually about half the price of a regular telegram, and you can send up to fifteen words. If you are anxious to let your president, congressperson, or senator know how you feel about a certain issue immediately, this is a great way to do it.

Sending Money

Sending money safely and quickly by telegram is discussed earlier in this chapter.

14 | Automobiles

Is there anyone out there who hasn't been car-crazy at one point or another? Buying a new car is beyond many budgets, but if any car, new or used, is in your immediate future, you'll profit from the tips in this chapter.

TERMS YOU SHOULD KNOW

ALTERNATOR: a device that is rotated by a belt from the engine to produce electricity and feed it to the *battery*.

BATTERY: stores electricity received from the *alternator* and feeds it to each of the parts of the car that runs on electricity.

BRAKE SYSTEM: the hydraulic system that applies pressure to your wheels to stop the car.

CARBURETOR: mixes air and fuel in the proper proportions and delivers the mixture through the intake *manifold* to the *cylinder* for burning.

CYLINDER: the can-shaped area in which the *piston* fits and in which fuel is burned to produce power.

CLUTCH: the device that allows you to shift gears by disconnecting and then reconnecting the engine and the *transmission*.

COIL: takes a small voltage from the *battery*, boosts it to a high voltage, and delivers it through the *distributor* to the *spark plugs*.

DISTRIBUTOR: accepts high-voltage electrical charges from the *coil* and sends them to each *spark plug* at the proper time for combusion in each *cylinder*.

ENGINE VALVES: intake valves open to admit air-fuel mixture into the *cylinder;* exhaust valves open to discharge burned gases into the tailpipe.

ELECTRICAL SYSTEM: the *alternator, battery,* wiring, and other devices that use electricity.

IGNITION SYSTEM: the part of the *electrical system* that allows the engine to fire; composed of the *battery, coil, distributor,* and *spark plugs.*

MANIFOLD: air-fuel mixture enters the *cylinder* through iron pipes called an intake manifold; exhaust gases exit through iron pipes called an exhaust manifold.

MUFFLER: a device mounted between the exhaust *manifold* and the tailpipe to reduce noise.

ODOMETER: registers the total miles driven and displays them on the speedometer face.

PISTON: travels up and down within the *cylinder* to compress the air-fuel mixture prior to combustion and to exhaust burned gases through the exhaust valves.

PISTON RINGS: rings around the piston to seal it so that fuel can't leak down the *cylinder* into the crankcase oil.

PCV VALVE (*positive crankcase ventilation valve*): recirculates unburned fuel to the *cylinder* to increase mileage and reduce pollution.

RADIATOR: cools the water that circulates through the engine to carry away excess heat.

SHOCK ABSORBER: a cylinder located near each wheel that absorbs the shock when the wheel passes over bumps or when the car is stopped suddenly.

SOLENOID: an electrical device that engages the *starter* to the engine when the ignition key is turned to the start position.

SPARK PLUGS: electrical devices mounted in the top of each *cylinder* to accept voltage from the *distributor* and produce a spark that ignites the fuel-air mixtures in the *cylinder.*

STARTER: a heavy-duty electric motor used to crank the engine in order to start it.

SUSPENSION SYSTEM: the system of springs, linkages, and *shock absorbers* that cushions the occupants of the car from bumps on the roadway.

TRANSMISSION: the set of gears that accepts power from the engine and transmits it to the drive shaft and ultimately to the wheels.

UNIVERSAL JOINT: the couplings that allow the drive shaft to rotate easily, thus providing power to the wheels even though the drive shaft may be slightly out of alignment.

WHEEL BEARINGS: ball bearings mounted on the end of each axle that reduce friction between the wheel and the axle.

BUYING A NEW CAR

Nothing can compare with that new-car look! Little compares with the size of the payments, either, but let's assume that you've found a way to afford a new car. How do you decide which one to buy?

Don't rush into buying a car. It'll be there tomorrow, and it'll be there after you've had time to investigate the alternatives.

Before You the Visit Showroom

The first thing to do is decide what make, size, and price car you want. Remember, there are many "hidden" costs in maintenance, financing, insurance, and depreciation (the market value your car loses each year). For price and performance reports of various models and sizes, check the library for *Consumer Reports, Changing Times, Mechanics Illustrated,* and *Motor Trend* magazines.

EPA Mileage Estimates

These are useful when comparing new cars. The Environmental Protection Agency runs tests each year on all new cars offered for sale. These tests are run by professional drivers, under laboratory conditions, so you probably won't get the high mileage figures published. However, the EPA estimates are useful to compare one car against another.

Options

You must also decide what options you want. Many options are purely matters of personal taste and the size of your pocketbook, but some can affect safety.

- A tinted windshield can reduce incoming light by 35 percent at dusk or after dark. This can be hazardous if you have poor night vision.
- A car with excessive power tends to be unstable and hard to

control in emergencies, according to the Center for Auto Safety.

- A rear-window defroster is well worth the price, for both safety and convenience.
- Front disk brakes are better than conventional drum brakes. They don't "grab" or have the instability of drum brakes. They also stay cooler and cut down on brake fading.
- Options that consume power, such as automatic transmission and power steering, also reduce mileage.

At the Showroom

The federal government requires auto manufacturers to provide information on performance. This information must be available at the dealership. Read it. You'll want to compare such factors as brake performance and acceleration. Make sure you know how long it takes to go from zero to 55 miles per hour. Also, find out how long it takes to go from 55 to 65 miles per hour when you are trying to pass. Then inspect the car itself:

- Check the spare tire. Is there one? Is it the same size as those on the car? Many manufacturers now make the spare tire an option, while others provide spare tires that are smaller than the regular tires. A smaller tire can be used in an emergency, but it can't be rotated with the others for everyday use.
- Check visibility from the driver's seat. Can you see well in strong sunlight? Do the windows distort vision? Are there blind spots? Could you see a small child near the car? Check the mirrors. The outside mirror should be located high enough so that you don't have to turn your head too far to see it. The inside mirror should not block forward vision.
- Sit in the driver's seat and fasten the belt. You should be able to reach all of the operating controls easily and comfortably, and be able to see them easily both day and night.
- Bring someone along with you to check the car's leg room and rear-seat riding comfort.
- Be sure you test drive the car you intend to buy, not just a "demonstrator."

Best Times to Buy

After you know what you want, shop around and compare prices. You can get the best deal twice a year—during the slow business months of winter and at the end of the model year. The length of time you plan to keep your car will determine when you want to buy it. If you plan to trade it in after only a few years, don't buy just before the new models are introduced in the fall. A car you buy in September is a "year old" by the next month, and loses a large percentage of its resale value immediately.

If you plan to keep the car for a while, August and September are good months to get discounts of 5 percent to 35 percent on American cars.

Sticker Prices

Remember that American cars rarely sell at their "sticker" prices. These stickers list the manufacturer's suggested list price, special preparation charges, transportation costs, and factory options. The dealer usually adds $300 to $800 on the wholesale cost of a medium-priced car. This is the area of bargaining in which each dealership is free to establish a final price—so check several dealers.

Trade It In or Sell It Yourself

Decide how you're going to sell your old car if you have one. You can sell it yourself, sell it to a used-car dealer, or trade it in to the new-car dealer and have its value deducted from the price of the new car. Although it's more work to sell your car yourself, it usually pays off. Advertise in the classified section of your local newspaper. You will probably get more money than you would by selling or trading it to a dealer.

Check the value of your old car by asking a bank or credit union to look it up for you in the *National Automobile Dealers' Association Official Used-Car Guide* or the *Kelley Blue Book*.

Option Prices

Options tend to be the highest profit-margin items sold by the dealer. One of the manufacturer's biggest advertising gimmicks is to give the "base" price and then add whopping increases for options such as side moldings, wheel covers, vinyl roofs, carpeting, radio, and so on.

You can usually beat the high prices of options by adding your own after you buy the car. You can buy molding strips and install them yourself for considerably less than the option price.

Car radios can usually be installed more cheaply by a shop that specializes in radio and stereo equipment. A radio from the car factory is generally 100 percent more expensive than one from a specialty shop. One option that is good to get from the factory, if needed, is an air conditioner. Most add-on air conditioners do not perform nearly as well as built-in types.

Warnings

When you've decided which car and which options you want, you are ready to talk with the dealer. Most dealers are reputable, but some are not. The following list tells you what to look out for:

- Low-balling: The salesperson quotes a low price, one he'll never actually give you, and then puts another on the sales contract, saying, "My boss won't let me go that low."
- High-balling: The salesperson quotes a high trade-in price, but later lowers it due to "manager's orders."
- Bait-and-switch advertising: The advertised car is not as good as it appeared to be, but for a higher price, you can have that "other car that is just what you want."
- Padding the tab: Dealers often add last-minute extras to the bill, such as a "protective" paint job or undercoating. Many of these features have already been provided and a look at the dealer's preparation checklist will let you know which ones.
- Bushing: The dealer will hike the price or lower a generous trade-in allowance after you have already put down a deposit.

Remember, if a salesperson makes you a promise on a deal, have him or her put it into writing. A verbal agreement will not do. If you are refused, then you know the promise is an empty one.

New-Car Warranties

All new cars are sold with written (express) warranties. By law, the warranties must be labeled "full" or "limited."

- "Full" Warranty: This means that a defective product will be fixed or replaced *free* within a specified time after your complaint. The warranty is good for anyone who owns the car during the specified period. If after a number of tries, the car proves to be unrepairable, you can have a new auto or your money back.

- "Limited" warranty: This covers only specific conditions and circumstances. The typical new-car warranty covers all parts of the car, except those listed as not covered. The warranty usually lasts twelve months or 12,000 miles, whichever comes first.
- Extended warranty: Often you may purchase an extended warranty that will increase the month and/or mileage limits. Make sure you know what your warranty covers.
- Dealer's reputation: Check your local Better Business Bureau to see how your dealer responds to the warranty-service requests of customers. A warranty isn't worth the paper it's printed on if the dealer doesn't perform the services adequately. It may be a good idea to buy your car from a dealer with a good service reputation. Even if you pay a little more for the car, it will be worth it later in warranty service.

BUYING A USED CAR

Unless you buy a used car carefully, you can encounter a number of problems, even if it runs well for the first few days. The transmission can start to lurch, the radiator can leak, the water pump can break down, the rearview mirror can fall off, and the front end can go out of alignment, to mention just a few possibilities. If you follow the guidelines in this section, you will greatly reduce your chances of buying a "lemon."

Before You Shop

Just as in buying a new car, your first stop when shopping for a used car is your local library. Check magazines like *Road and Track, Motor Trend, Car and Driver, Consumer Digest,* and *Consumer Reports* (the April 1977 issue is full of information). Also check the 1978–79 *Consumer Reports Guide to Used Cars.* Read about the tests performed on the cars, and compare the data. Many of these magazines test used as well as new cars. Be diligent in your research. Remember, you're about to lay out a lot of money, and you want something good in return. Librarians will help you find these magazines.

You can always change your mind later, but I strongly advise that you choose the make of car you want *before* you actually go out and look for it. Your bank should have a *Kelley Blue Book* or the *National Automobile Dealers' Association Used-Car Guide.* These books give suggested retail and wholesale prices for all cars made in the past five years, which should give you a good idea of the approximate value of various cars. Of course, the car's over-all condition will affect the price.

Remember that the price of a used car is negotiable. If you decide that you have found your car, don't give the asking price. Make an offer.

Safety Defects in Used Cars

Some used cars may have been recalled for safety defects by the manufacturer, but the previous owner may not have returned the car for repair. Call the National Highway Traffic Safety Administration, Office of Consumer Services (1-202-426-0671 or 1-202-426-0670), and give them the make, model, year, and vehicle identification number (VIN) of the car to obtain a report of all defects and and recalls for that make and model.

Mileage

Mileage is another consideration, but mileage alone is not the most important factor to consider in a used car. The "average" car will have been driven about 10,000 to 12,000 miles per year. If the car you're interested in passes the checklist on page 178 and falls into this mileage range, it should be just what you want. Cars formerly owned by the police force, rental agencies, or corporate fleets are generally in good condition since they have received regular maintenance. Cars owned by taxi companies usually have too many miles on them to be of much use for long.

Where to Find a Used Car

There are three good places to buy a used car: from a private party, from a used-car dealer, or from a new-car dealer.

Buying from a private party means buying either from a person you know or from people who advertise in the classified section of the newspaper. The advantage of buying from a private party is that you usually get the lowest possible price. The disadvantages are that there is no warranty (any repairs needed will be at your expense) and there is a possibility that the vehicle may have been stolen. Make sure the title matches the car's identification number (VIN, explained later). If you can't find it, call a dealer that sells that type of car and ask where it is located on the car.

Buying from a used-car dealer has advantages in that the prices are generally lower than those of a new-car dealer, and your older used car will normally be accepted as a trade-in. However, any warranty you get from a used-car dealer is likely to be limited, so you take your chances on the car's condition. Most used-car dealers sell their cars "as is." One precaution would be to buy from a dealer who displays the emblem of one of the trade-in associations: the National Automobile Dealers Association or the National Independent Auto Dealers Association.

Finally, you can buy a used car from a new-car dealer who sells cars that have been traded in to him. Generally, prices are higher, but a warranty is usually offered.

How to Check Out a Used Car

You don't have to be a master mechanic to find a car that is in good shape. All you have to do is inspect it carefully. To make this inspection, take a pen and paper, a friend, and the following checklist with you. Always check a car in daylight. Night and rain conceal even the worst defects.

• Check the paint job and over-all appearance for an indication of how the car was treated. Ripples in the paint or repainted spots may indicate that the car has been in an accident. Check to see if the car has been repainted by matching the body color with that of the trunk, door posts, or engine firewall. Also, check seat-cushion springs and the gas pedal for signs of wear. Excessive wear indicates that the car has spent many hard miles on the road.

• Look for signs of rust, especially in the wheel wells and around the rocker panels under the doors. Rust is like a cancer. Once it starts, it's almost impossible to stop. It weakens the car's basic structure.

• Check the tires carefully. Uneven tread wear can indicate that the wheels are out of alignment. If the car is relatively new, all four tires should be of the same brand. If they aren't, the car may have a bad ball-joint suspension or another alignment problem.

- Shake each front wheel hard. Put your hands on the top of the tire and shake the wheel in and out. If it "clunks," is loose, or has a lot of free play, the wheel bearings or suspension joints will have to be replaced.
- Check the shock absorbers by pushing down on each corner of the car a few times and then letting go. The car should bounce *once* and stop. If it bounces more than once, the shocks must be replaced. Look at the shocks. If they look wet, they leak and will have to be replaced. Driving on worn shocks is hazardous as it can cause loss of control when cornering.
- Climb inside and check the operating controls. Make sure all the lights work. Check turn signals, four-way flashers, windshield wipers, inside light, radio, headlights, high beams, brake lights, and tail lights.
- Press the brake pedal for one minute. If the pedal slowly starts to sink in or goes all the way to the floor, there may be a brake-fluid leak.
- Make sure all the windows roll up and down easily and that the doors close tightly, lock, and don't sag when they are opened.
- Check the door, trunk, hood, and glove compartment latches in their locked and unlocked positions.
- Look under the hood for oil, water, and gas leaks. Check all hoses and belts for wear. The radiator coolant should not be oily or rusty.

  When you check the oil level, the oil dipstick should not have any water droplets on it. Water indicates a blown head gasket.

  In a car with automatic transmission, the transmission dipstick should show a bright red fluid. Fluid that is orange or black or that smells like varnish indicates a damaged transmission.
- Start the car. Have a friend check the exhaust while you race the engine. White exhaust is normal, black indicates that the carburetor is untuned, and blue indicates that the engine is worn.
- Ask your friend to watch the tires as you drive away. The wheels should be in line. If both the front and rear wheels are out, the car's frame is probably bent because the car has been in an accident.

- Test the brakes by going about 35 miles per hour and then, after making sure no one is behind you, hitting the brakes hard. Don't lock the wheels, however. If you start to skid, let up on the brakes. Repeat this at least three times. The brake pedal should not become spongy. It should stay well above the floor. Also, the car should not swerve when the brakes are applied or as the car is slowing down. Make sure you have your seat belt fastened for this maneuver!
- Check the play in the steering wheel. It shouldn't be extremely loose or tight.
- Drive the car in all its gears. An automatic transmission should shift smoothly and quietly, with no lurching or laboring. A manual transmission should not chatter, rattle, or stick in gear.

  To check the clutch on a car with manual transmission, put the car's emergency brake on and start the engine with the clutch pedal depressed. Now put the car in first gear and slowly release the clutch. The engine should stall and quit running. If it does not, the clutch is bad.
- Drive backwards and forwards several feet and listen for strange noises! A clanking sound may indicate a bad universal joint.
- Check to see whether the car accelerates smoothly. If the car can't get to high speeds quickly, it may need an overhaul.
- Drive over a rough, bumpy road to see if the suspension is good. Don't buy the car if it's hard to control.
- Try to find a long hill. Check the piston rings by driving down the hill. Before you get to the bottom, step hard on the gas and look for smoke in the rearview mirror. Black smoke indicates a gas-air mixture that is too rich which wastes fuel. Blue smoke usually means the car is burning oil due to a worn engine.
- When you return from your test drive, let the car idle for a few minutes. Look *under the car* for dripping gas, water, or oil. Reddish oil is transmission fluid. Black oil is engine oil. Gas drips evaporate, leaving a brownish stain.
- Once again, check *under the hood* for leaks of oil, water, or gas.

If, after these tests, the car seems to be acceptable, you may want to do one last thing. Take the car to a diagnostic-test center, or to *your* mechanic. Have it looked over and get any repair estimates in writing. This will usually run between $15 and $30, and is well worth the money. It could prevent you from buying a lemon.

Warnings

Have another look at "Warnings" in the new-car section in this chapter. All of those tricks can also be tried with used cars. In addition, it's not unusual to run into a used-car dealer who engages in the practice of "doping." This is what happens when you are told that the used car you are interested in has been "totally reconditioned." It seems fine to you, but after a few days, the car develops a variety of problems. This is because the dealer used various methods to temporarily hide the faults. You get stuck while the dealer gets rich.

Here's how to avoid falling into these traps:

- Have a mechanic check the car *before* you buy it.
- Try to get at least a thirty-day full warranty making the dealer responsible for the costs of all repairs needed.
- If you can't get a full warranty, try to get the dealer to go fifty-fifty with you. During a specific time period, usually a month, you and the dealer split repair costs.
- Make sure *all* promises and agreements the dealer makes with you are put in writing.
- Don't buy a car whose price is far below that of others in the same category. It is probably a lemon.
- Never buy a car without a test drive. Avoid dealers who say test drives are not allowed. They are hiding something.
- If you have problems with your contract or you think the seller is breaking the law, contact the Department of Motor Vehicles in your state.

Vehicle Identification

Both the title and the registration of the car you buy carry a Vehicle Identification Number (VIN). The VIN on the title and on the registration must match the VIN on the car itself. This number is usually on the dashboard in front of the driver's seat where the windshield meets the dash. It's easiest to see from outside the car. If the numbers don't match, you don't want the car. It's stolen!

Title and Registration

When buying a used car, you should receive the title, properly signed by the seller before a notary public (a person who is authorized by the government to certify or attest to documents). Having the title "notarized" means that the title is signed in the presence of a notary public. Notary publics can be found by consulting the Yellow Pages of your telephone book or at your local bank.

Once you have the notarized title and registration, you must contact your local Department of Motor Vehicles in order to have the new title and registration recorded in your name.

SAFETY EQUIPMENT

You are not ready to take your car out on the road until you have safety equipment and tools, which you should keep in the car at all times. Here is a list of basic equipment:

- Spare tire
- Cross-shaped lug wrench (easier to handle than a jack-handle wrench)
- Liquid wrench (loosens rusty lugs)
- Mini-compressor (inflates your tire until you can get to a repair shop)
- Flashlight
- Flares and/or reflectors
- Small shovel (if you live in a region where it snows)
- Equipment to create traction for snowy and icy conditions (These can be metal or rubber grids, pieces of carpeting, sand, or even kitty litter.)
- Tools, including a hammer, screwdriver, pliers, and a rubber mallet

Other equipment some people like to keep includes rope, extra fanbelts (some repair shops don't carry them), and booster cables. Booster cables can be dangerous, however, so be sure you know how to use them. If you travel a great deal and can afford it, you might want to belong to an organization like the American Automobile Association (AAA), which provides assistance in emergencies as well as travel information.

SERVICE AND REPAIR

Now that you're a proud automobile owner, you should know how to "keep that Rolls rolling." This section will explain preventative maintenance, finding repair shops, and having satisfactory repairs made.

Checking for Problems

The first step in preventative car care is to *read your owner's manual.* It gives such information as how often oil should be changed, new spark plugs put in, and so on. After reading your owner's manual, you can make some simple checks.

- Battery: Are the cables rusty or corroded? If so, clean them by putting baking soda on them, then pouring water over the soda. Make sure the cables are tight around the battery posts. Check the water level by pulling off the vent caps and looking at the water. It should cover the core and touch the "full" line in the neck of the hole. Fill, if needed, preferably with distilled water. In hot weather, do this once a week. Once a month is fine in cold weather.
    TROUBLE SIGNS: battery that frequently needs water; sluggish starting; dim lights when engine isn't running.
- Oil: If you run your engine with too little oil, major engine damage can occur. Prevent this by regularly checking your oil level. Pull out the oil dipstick, wipe it clean with a rag, replace it firmly in its hole, and pull it out again. Check to see if the oil is on the "full" line. If not, add oil until it is full. Always check the oil with the engine turned off.
    TROUBLE SIGNS: red oil-warning light; showing little or no pressure on oil-pressure gauge.
- Transmission fluid: Use the transmission dipstick, usually located at the rear of the engine, to check the fluid level according to the procedure explained in your owner's manual. Most automatic transmissions should be checked with the engine running and the gears in park.
    TROUBLE SIGNS: jerky, uneven acceleration; growling noises; whining while driving; sticking gears.
- Cooling system: With the engine *cold,* open the radiator pressure cap and check the fluid level. It should be over the radia-

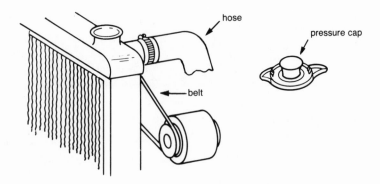

hose

pressure cap

belt

Make sure the radiator is cold before you try to remove the pressure cap.

The way your tires wear can indicate that they are over- or underinflated, or that the wheels are out of balance or alignment.

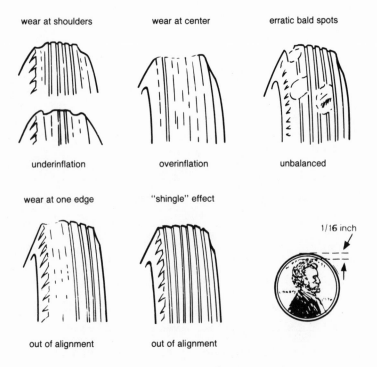

wear at shoulders

wear at center

erratic bald spots

underinflation

overinflation

unbalanced

wear at one edge

"shingle" effect

1/16 inch

out of alignment

out of alignment

tor core and about an inch below the top of the filler neck. Add antifreeze or water as needed to fill up the system. Check the radiator hoses for frays or other signs of wear. Have them replaced if needed. Check all belts for fraying. Grab the belts, push them in, and pull them out. They should have no more than ½-inch play in the longest segment of the belts' travel. Have a mechanic check the tension if you're unsure of it.

TROUBLE SIGNS: temperature gauge reads high; you need to add liquid frequently.

- Tires: Correct tire pressure is necessary for good tire mileage, gas mileage, and responsive steering. Buy a good tire gauge, and use it at least once a month. Inspect the tire treads. Wear on the edges indicates underinflation, while wear in the center means too much air pressure. Look for cuts, bruises, or tread separations. A simple check for tread wear is to insert a penny into the tread. If the tread does not cover the top of Lincoln's head, you have less than ¹⁄₁₆ inch of tread left and you need new tires.

TROUBLE SIGNS: pulling to the right or left; uneven braking; excessive squealing on corners.

There are other items on your car that you should know about, although it will usually be necessary for a mechanic to check out and repair them:

- Brakes: Brakes are usually self-adjusting unless something mechanical goes wrong. You may occasionally need to add brake fluid. Check your owner's manual for instructions. Have faulty brakes repaired *as soon as possible,* since brakes that do not function properly are extremely dangerous.

TROUBLE SIGNS: spongy feeling when you press brake pedal; long pedal movement; scraping noises; pulling to one side when car stops or slows down.

- Carburetor: The carburetor mixes gasoline with air and sends the mixture to the engine cylinders to be burned. It requires periodic checking. Items such as the automatic choke and idle speed should be adjusted with every tune-up.

TROUBLE SIGNS: hard starting; hesitation when you press gas pedal; stalling-out at stops; idling too fast or too slow; sluggishness at road speeds; a tendency to "run on" after you turn off the ignition, also called "dieseling."

- Engine valves: The valves permit the air-fuel mixture from the carburetor to enter the engine cylinders, and they allow waste gases inside the cylinder to escape. Your owner's manual should tell you how often to have your valves adjusted.

TROUBLE SIGNS: loss of power; light clattering or tapping noise; hard starting, especially in the cold; an uneven feel to engine performance.

• Ignition system: The ignition system consists of the battery, the alternator or generator, coil, distributor, spark plugs, and wires. The whole system channels an electric current to the spark plugs, igniting the air-fuel mixture in the cylinders. In a tune-up, the entire ignition system should be checked.

TROUBLE SIGNS: hard starting; uneven acceleration; loss of power at high speeds; rough idle; partial or complete "miss" in one or more of the cylinders, causing rough performance and severe loss of power.

• Clutch: In a car with a manual transmission, the clutch is used to change from one gear to another. Its linkages and fluid levels should be checked in accordance with the owner's manual specifications.

TROUBLE SIGNS: clashing of the gears when shifting; a "slipping" feeling during start-up or acceleration; "chattering" when starting to move.

• Front suspension: The front suspension of your car should be aligned at all times, but rough roads and driving conditions can cause it to go out of line.

TROUBLE SIGNS: uneven tire wear; pulling to one side or the other during driving, even when tire pressure and wheel balance are correct (see illustrations on page 184).

Choosing a Repair Shop

When you run into problems that are beyond your ability to diagnose and correct—and we all do—it's important to find a mechanic and a shop you can trust. Too many people spend good money on "repairs" that don't correct the problem. There are several types of repair shops to choose from. Any large metropolitan area will have the following:

• Car dealers: You will usually go to the dealer when your car is still under warranty. The dealer is normally the most expensive for replacement parts and labor charges.
• Gas stations: Stations have long hours, but usually do only general jobs, such as lubrications, oil changes, tune-ups,

shocks, brakes, mufflers, hoses, tires, batteries, lights, filters, and windshield wipers.

- Independent garages: These are cheaper than dealerships, but highly trained mechanics charge more for labor than gas-station mechanics. They do all the things gas-station mechanics do, as well as suspensions, springs, ball joints, and electrical systems. Many do major engine overhauls, too.
- Muffler shops: These repair and replace mufflers, exhaust pipes, brackets, and manifolds. Local muffler shops are usually less expensive than national chain shops and often give the same lifetime guarantee.
- Brake shops: These specialize in relining brakes and removing and machining disks and drums.
- Tire stores: Besides selling and installing tires, they often replace shocks, give front-end alignments, reline brakes, change oil, and lubricate engines.
- Automatic transmission shops: These diagnose and repair transmission problems.
- Tune-up centers: They provide tune-ups only, usually at much lower prices than dealerships, gas stations, or independent garages.
- Air-conditioning shops: Excellent for air-conditioner installation if it's an add-on unit, they have the proper tools and usually guarantee their work for a considerable period of time.
- Phone-a-mechanic: This is a relatively new service. You call the mechanic and he comes to where you are instead of your going to where he is. The prices are usually low, but guarantees are not readily available. All guarantees should be put in writing.

Choosing the right shop will help you to get good, reliable service for your car. Here are some tips for finding one:

- Ask friends for recommendations. The best advertisement any shop can have is a satisfied customer.
- When checking out a repair shop, find out if its mechanics are certified and licensed. The National Institute for Automotive Service Excellence (NIASE) gives voluntary tests to mechanics on such subjects as tune-ups, engine repairs, brakes, transmissions, front ends, suspension systems, and others. The tests are comprehensive, and anyone who passes is qualified in

that field. You can be assured that someone wearing the NIASE patch for a specific subject knows what he is doing.

You can get a directory of NIASE mechanics by writing to:

National Institute for Automotive Service Excellence
Suite 515
1825 K Street NW
Washington, D.C. 20006

- Check to see if the shop will back repairs with a guarantee. A typical guarantee might be 3,000 miles or two months, whichever comes first.
- Ask for a written estimate. It's important to have one so you won't pay more than you expect to. Write on the estimate that you would like to be called in advance for approval if additional work needs to be done. Have the estimate signed by the person who wrote it, and keep a copy for yourself.
- Remember that each shop should be looked at carefully. Your decision as to where you have your car repaired should not be based on price alone, but on all the criteria listed in this section.

Explaining the Problem to a Mechanic

When you describe the problem to a mechanic, make sure you tell him what is wrong as clearly as possible. Tell him what your car is doing or not doing, and let him determine the cause. That's his job. Be specific. Tell him what happens and when. Does it happen at idle? At high speeds? When you first start the engine? Is it continuous or occasional? Did it happen gradually or suddenly? Does it happen in heavy traffic? Are there unusual noises? Clunking? Grinding?

By stating *what* is happening instead of trying to say *why*, you will help the mechanic find the real problem.

A good mechanic is a pearl beyond price. Once you've found one, hang on to him! Treat him well by recommending him to your friends. Have them use your name when they stop by so he'll know you trust him enough to send him additional business. He'll value you more as a customer, and you'll be able to look forward to years of dependable and honest service.

Help with Faulty Repairs

- Dealer repair shops: If you're at a dealership, talk to the owner about unsatisfactory repairs. If you get no response from him, find the nearest district office of the company by looking on your warranty papers or in your owner's manual, and write to them or call them. Ask to talk to the customer-service representative. If this fails, you will probably want to contact AUTOCAP, or the Automotive Consumer Action Panel, in your area. This agency claims to successfully solve 75 percent to 80 percent of all its cases.

• Private garages: If you're at a private garage, complain to the owner. If he does not respond, contact the Automotive Service Council, Center for Auto Safety, or your local consumer protection agency.

The Automotive Service Council has local chapters all over the country. The agency will try to have one of its mechanics check your car, and determine whether the mechanic was at fault. If he was, they will put pressure on him to fix it. Check the phone book for your local chapter.

The Center for Auto Safety was founded by Ralph Nader. It is interested in finding widespread problem areas, and your letter will help them. Mail your complaint to:

Center for Auto Safety
1223 Dupont Circle Building
Washington, D.C. 20036

• Service stations: If you're having trouble with a service station, complain to the national company that owns the station's franchise.

Avoid Overheating

If you are stopped in traffic and the temperature gauge needle is in the danger zone, take these steps, one after the other. You may not need to take them all:

• Shift to neutral and press the accelerator one quarter of the way down. Be sure the air conditioner is turned off, and stay at least one car length behind the car ahead.

• Open the windows and turn on the heater. This will make you uncomfortable, but may prevent a boilover.

• As soon as possible, pull over, turn the engine off, open the hood, and let it cool. *Do not try to remove the radiator cap while it is hot!*

• After the engine cools, drive slowly to a service station to identify the cause of overheating, unless you have lost radiator coolant by a boilover. If you have lost coolant, add enough water to drive to a service station for repairs and new coolant.

Fuel-Saving Checklist

* Drive at reasonable speeds. It has been proved that the average car gets 21 percent better mileage at 55 miles per hour than it does at 70 miles per hour.
* Accelerate smoothly. This saves gas as well as your engine and tires.
* Drive at a steady pace. Try to avoid stop-and-go traffic.
* Don't weave in and out of traffic lanes.
* Don't let the engine idle for more than a minute while you are temporarily stopped. It takes less gas to restart the engine than to let it run for one minute.

New Cars on Grass

New cars (1975 to the present) have catalytic converters that can reach 1200° F. and usually reach that temperature *after* the car is turned off. The heat can ignite grass, weeds, grease, and other flammable substances under your car.

Tire Tips

If you're buying two new tires for your car, put them on the rear for better traction and handling. A single new tire should also be put on the rear. The other rear tire should have the most tread depth of the remaining three. Never use a radial tire with any other type of tire on the same axle.

ACCIDENTS

In 1902, there were only two automobiles in the state of Iowa, and they met in a head-on collision in Dubuque! Perhaps they were setting the trend for what was to become the largest cause of property damage and personal injury in the country—auto accidents. It is calculated that every year, one out of four drivers in the United States will be involved in an accident.

Driving defensively is the best way to avoid becoming a highway statistic. If your mental "caution sign" is on yellow whenever you're behind the wheel, you'll drive much more safely and arrive at your destination better rested.

If You Are Involved in an Accident

- Stop immediately. Keep calm. Help anyone who might be injured (see Chapter 10). Move cars off the road or have someone route traffic around them until the police take charge.
- Exchange your name, address, phone number, driver's license number, license-tag number, and auto-insurance company name with the driver of the other car.

After an Accident

Most states require an immediate report, either written or oral, for any accident causing injury or death. A formal written report completely detailing the accident is usually required in addition to the immediate report. Laws vary from state to state, so check. You can get all the information you need from the Motor Vehicle Division of the Department of Transportation in your state or from your *Driver's Test Manual.*

If You're a Bystander

- Park your car in a safe place. If possible, turn off the ignition on the cars involved in the accident. Give first aid to the injured (see Chapter 10). Remember, *do not* move anyone who is injured unless his or her life depends on it.
- Summon police, and, if necessary, an ambulance. Direct traffic around the accident. Report what you've done to the police when they arrive, and let them suggest any other help you can give.

Information to Keep in Your Glove Compartment

Any accident, even one with no injuries, shakes you up, and you're liable to forget some of the things you should remember.

Fill out a card containing the following information. You'll need it if you're in an accident. Keep it in your glove compartment.

Car color ——————— Make ———— Year ————
Car registration number ————————————————
Driver's license number ————————————————
Your name ——————————————————————
Address ——————————————————————
Phone number ——————————————————————

In case of injury notify _____
Address _____
Phone number _____

Health insurance company _____
Car insurance company _____
Insurance agent _____
Phone number _____

Record information about the other person involved in the accident on the back of the card. Make it up so that you can easily fill in the information you will need:

Other car
Car color _____ Make _____ Year _____
Car registration number _____
Owner's name _____
Address _____
Phone number _____

Driver's name _____
Address _____
Phone number _____
License number _____

Insurance company _____
Phone number _____
Agent's names _____
Phone number _____

Witnesses
Name _____ Address _____ Phone number __
Name _____ Address _____ Phone number __
Name _____ Address _____ Phone number __

Police officer's name _____
Badge number _____

15 | Travel

Time is money. The greater hurry you are in to get somewhere, the more it's liable to cost you. So let's look at some travel alternatives, from hiking to flying.

HIKING

The very word conjures up visions of stalwart bodies, heavy laden, striding purposefully over mountain and through forest, sleeping by the trail. And it does pay to be trim and fit if you're planning an extended hike. One of the best ways to get in that kind of shape is to take shorter hikes and work up to the long one. It also pays to plan your hike carefully.

Most schools and colleges have hiking societies that encourage new members and sponsor trips and classes. If you don't have any hiking clubs nearby, there are many hiking and backpacking books available in the library, and if hiking is new to you it's good to read up on it before you buy equipment. You'll also want to get an idea of the various trails so you won't choose one that's too difficult. You can send for applications for topographical maps that show the hiking trails to:

U.S. Geological Survey
Box 25286
Denver Federal Center
Denver, Colo. 80225

Or you can get hiking maps in any national park from the Forest Service.

There are also several national organizations that can send

you more information. Here are the addresses of one on each coast.

Sierra Club
530 Bush Street
San Francisco, Ca. 94108

Appalachian Trail Conference
Box 236
Harper's Ferry, W. Va. 25425

Camping outfitters usually have a library section that offers many useful pamphlets and books for beginning and experienced hikers. They provide tips on backpack selection and zone packing, lists of recommended first-aid and survival items, foods, and other useful information. Check *America's Backpacking Book,* written by Raymond Bridge, published by Charles Scribner's Sons (New York, 1973) and *Outdoor Living—Problems, Solutions and Guidelines,* published by Tacoma Mountain Rescue Unit, P.O. Box 696, Tacoma, Wa. 98401.

However you outfit and wherever you hike, be sure to follow the cardinal rules of hiking. File a hike plan with some responsible person. List your starting point, expected check points, and the finish point. Show the date you expect to be at each. List the names of all those going with you. Don't overstay. You won't want a search party looking for you if it's unnecessary.

Take survival gear, including a good first-aid kit, compass, knife, matches wrapped in plastic, whistle, flashlight, and dehydrated food.

Leave nothing behind but your footprints. Carry out refuse. Don't bury it for some animal to dig up. Leave your camping area cleaner than you found it.

BIKE TRAILS

There are bikeways all across America, and many regional tourist offices have free maps of their bikeways. If you are interested in buying maps and guidebooks on the five sections of the Transamerica Bicycle Trail—West Coast Cascades, Rocky Mountains, Plains/Ozarks, Bluegrass, and Appalachians—write for information to:

Bikecentennial
P.O. Box 8308
Missoula, Mont. 59807

Some handy tips while biking:

- Use toe clips to save energy.
- Clothes
  1. Wear bright clothes.
  2. Cover your arms to avoid sunburn.
  3. Wear sunglasses to protect your eyes from wind and insects.
  4. Wear gloves to help prevent callouses.
- Wrap the handlebars with neoprene rubber and tape. This will allow you to move your hands into different positions and avoid tiring.
- Use maps and guidebooks and schedule a definite trip plan that people at home know about so that they can contact you if necessary.
- Don't use a backpack. It is difficult to balance on long-distance rides. Carry gear on the back of the bike or on the handlebars. Keep a small bag for valuables on your handlebars so it will be handy. If you leave your bike it will be easy to take with you.
- Be sure to plan days to just rest and clean up. Ride four or five days, then rest. Stay at hostels or in campgrounds.

AUTOMOBILE TRAVEL

Skyrocketing fuel costs have driven the price of automobile travel almost as high as air travel, but carrying paying passengers can cut your costs significantly. Some local radio stations have ride lines with taped messages advertising for riders and rides, and many colleges have travel bulletin boards that post want ads for rides.

Using a drive-away service can cut costs also. You'll find such services listed in the Yellow Pages under "Automobile-Driving" or "Drive-away." Drive-away is actually a dual service. Someone who wants his car driven to another location will often utilize a drive-away service. Then someone like you, who wants to drive to that location calls the drive-away service and is matched up with the car. Some services require that you pay for fuel and oil. Some provide insurance; others require that you buy it. All require that you have a valid driver's license and be at least eighteen years old (often twenty-one).

BUS AND TRAIN

There are still some travel bargains on buses. Call each of the large bus companies in your area and inquire about special rates, excursions, and similar money savers. Most bus companies offer a pass that allows unlimited travel during a specific time period.

Trains are not always the most convenient way of travel and it can be frustrating just trying to get a ticket agent to answer the phone, but there's something romantic about thundering through the night in the great iron horse. Call Amtrak for information, or try a travel agent.

AIR TRAVEL

Since deregulation, the major airlines have announced a bewildering array of cost-saving air fares. If you plan to travel by air, call each of the airlines serving your community and inquire about available discounts. Flying is an exciting way to travel but can be confusing at first.

A free booklet tells you how to buy tickets, handle baggage, and simplify travel by air. Send a self-addressed stamped envelope (# 10 large size) to:

Air Transport Association
Department FC
1709 New York Avenue NW
Washington, D.C. 20006

Luggage

If your luggage is lost or damaged or sent to Timbuctu, report it to the airlines immediately. When luggage is lost on domestic flights (inside the United States), the airlines are required to give you enough money to buy the necessities that were lost. If your baggage is damaged or permanently lost, airlines must pay its reasonable value up to $750. Demand reimbursement, or you won't get it!

Canceled or Delayed Flights

If your flight is canceled, the airlines are required to get you on the next available flight to your destination. There is no extra fee for this service.

If your flight is delayed for more than four hours, the airlines are required to compensate you. Depending on the time of day, they must provide hotel accommodations, meals, and transportation to a hotel. The airlines must allow you to place at no cost either a three-minute long-distance telephone call or a fifteen word telegram to your destination. A pamphlet at the ticket counter, called *CAB rules Tariff No. 142 Rule 380* tells you what the airlines are expected to do in case of delay.

Bumping

Because airlines never know how many people with confirmed reservations will show up for a flight, they sometimes overbook, and too many people appear for the flight. Then the airlines have to "bump," or leave behind, some of the travelers who were supposed to be on the flight. Airlines are required to give those bumped a statement of their rights (refunds, new reservations, hotel rooms, meals, and so on). To avoid being bumped, check in at the gate (not the ticket counter) at least ten minutes before departure. Your reservation can be canceled if you are not at the gate at that time.

INEXPENSIVE PLACES TO STAY

Where you decide to stay is a function of how much you can afford to spend. If you are an informal traveler you might want to consider a hostel.

Hostels

Young travelers can stay at a hostel overnight for two to four dollars. If you want to see the United States inexpensively, join American Youth Hostels. For a small fee, you have access to guided group travel and places to stay if you're traveling alone or with a friend. If you're a biker, this organization will be a great help. For more information call 703 592-3271 or write:

American Youth Hostels, Inc.
National Campus
Delaplane, Va. 22025

Student Travel Services

The Council on International Educational Exchange (CIEE) offers a book called *Where to Stay, U.S.A. from 50¢ to $10.00 a*

Night ($2.95). You can check your library for a copy, or write to:
CIEE Student Travel Services
777 United Nations Plaza
New York, N.Y. 10017

National Parks and Forests

For detailed information about these parks, write for *Directories for National Services Visitor's Accommodations Facilities and Services* (pamphlet number 024-005-00648-6, $1.05). This pamphlet is written by the National Park Services and can be obtained by writing to this address:
United States Government Printing Office
Washington, D.C. 20402
For information on campgrounds in the United States, consult *Campground and Trailer Guide, National Edition.* It is published by Rand McNally and revised annually.

MOTELS AND HOTELS

If you can afford to stay in motels or hotels, we can recommend two good guides. *Hotel and Travel Index* ($2.00) can be obtained from:
Ziff-Davis Publishing Company
1 Park Avenue,
New York, N.Y. 10016
You can order *Hotel and Motel Redbook* ($25.00) from:
American Hotel and Motel Association
888 7th Avenue
New York, N.Y. 10019
Your local library and most travel agents have copies of these guides. Browsing through them while planning a trip can be enjoyable and rewarding. To better understand what the notations in these publications mean, here's an explanation of the various plans.

- American Plan: "(AP)" means that the rate includes room plus three meals daily.
- Modified American Plan: "(MAP)" means that the rate includes room, breakfast, and one other meal daily.
- Bermuda Plan: "(BP)" means that the rate includes room and full breakfast.

- Bed and Breakfast Plan: "(B&B)" means the same as the Bermuda Plan.
- Continental Plan: "(CP)" means that the rate includes room plus a coffee and roll breakfast only.
- European Plan: "(EP)" means the rate is for the room only. All meals are extra.

TRAVEL AGENTS

Travel agents do not charge you for their services, so don't hesitate to ask them for help if you are planning a trip. They provide information and make reservations and even help you schedule your itinerary. They are paid by the hotels, airlines, and travel services. Be sure you deal with a reputable tour or travel agent. If you are in doubt, call the Better Business Bureau to check an agent's complaint history.

PASSPORTS

If you visit our neighbors to the north and south, you'll find that neither Canada nor Mexico requires a passport. You will, however, need some proof that you're a United States citizen.

When traveling to other foreign countries, a passport is an absolute requirement. Apply early, at least six weeks before your expected departure.

It's best to call the passport office and ask what will be required before going there in person. In general, you'll need some personal identification, a true copy of your registered birth certificate (one that has the imprint of the state seal), two passport-sized photographs of yourself, and twelve dollars for the fee.

You may unexpectedly have a chance to travel abroad and find yourself without the time to get your birth certificate or wait for normal passport processing. If you use express mail service (see Chapter 13) you can get your birth certificate within twenty-four hours. The passport office might not volunteer the information, but it has a service, which costs only three dollars, that can shorten the time necessary to issue your passport from weeks to a few days. Ask for their "expediting service."

A Final Word

A few days ago, I was having my hair done at the local beauty school. During our conversation, my hairdresser mentioned that she was training to be a beautician because the money was good but she really wanted to be an actress. For years, she had nursed this dream but had never auditioned for anything because she was afraid of failure.

When I told her that each of us, including me, has failed many times over, the idea was new to her. The thought of failing at something important had kept her from even trying! After listening to a recital of my own failures and the later successes that they made possible, she began to see that *trying* is important. Trying builds us up so we can achieve success.

As I was leaving, a much happier young woman told me that she had decided to audition for a part in a play to be presented by our community theater.

And so, my final word to you is a simple one. Never, but never, be afraid to fail. Talk to any successful person in any field. Read about the lives of famous people. You'll find the same thread running through them all: if they had been afraid to fail, they *never* would have succeeded.

Believe in yourself.

Further Reading

1. Training for the Job

Career Guidance Education: Exploring Careers. Washington, D.C.: U.S. Government Printing Office, published biannually.

Occupational Outlook Handbook. Washington, D.C.: U.S. Department of Labor, published biannually.

Our Vocational Training Can Guarantee You the Job of a Lifetime, Washington, D.C.: U.S. Federal Trade Commission, 1978.

2. Getting the Job

Bolles, Richard N. *What Color is Your Parachute?* Berkeley: Ten Speed Press, 1978.

Working For the U.S.A. Washington, D.C.: U.S. Civil Service Commission, 1975.

4. Managing Money

Blodgett, Richard E. *New York Times Book of Money.* New York: New York Times Book Co., 1976.

Consumer Buying Guide. Mount Vernon: Consumers Union of the U.S., published annually.

Smith, Carlton. *The Time-Life Book of Family Income.* Alexandria: Time-Life Books, 1969.

Understanding Taxes '79. Washington, D.C.: Internal Revenue Service, 1979.

5. Banking

Porter, Sylvia. *The Money Book*. New York: Doubleday, 1979.
Troelstrup, A.W. *The Consumer in American Society*. New York: McGraw Hill, 1974.

6. Credit and Loans

Consumer Handbook to Credit Protection Laws. Washington, D.C.: U.S. Federal Reserve System, 1979.

7. Insurance

Consumer Buying Guide, 1979. New York: Consumers Union of the U.S., 1978.
Mayerson, Allen L. *Introduction to Insurance*. New York: Macmillan, 1962.

8. Clothing

Head, Edith. *How to Dress for Success*. New York: Random House, 1967.
Picken, Mary. *Textile Industry and Fashion Dictionary*. New York: Funk and Wagnalls, 1973.

9. Health and Fitness

An Introduction to Physical Fitness: The President's Council on Physical Fitness and Sports. Washington, D.C.: U.S. Superintendant of Documents, 1979.
Davis, Adele. *Let's Eat Right to Keep Fit*. New York: Harcourt Brace Jovanovich, 1970.
Zohman, Lenore R. M.D., *Exercise Your Way to Fitness and Heart Health*. Englewood Cliffs: A Public Service Publication by Mazola Corn Oil, a unit of Best Foods, CPC International, Inc., 1974.

10. Emergencies

In Time of Emergency. Washington, D.C.: Department of Defense, 1976.
The Ship's Medical Chest and Medical Aid at Sea. Washington D.C.: U.S. Department of Health, Education and Welfare, 1978.

11. Consumer and Legal Aids

Help: The Useful Almanac. Washington, D.C.: Consumer News Inc., 1978.

The Compleat California Consumer Catalogue. Sacramento: California Department of Consumer Affairs, 1977.

12. Government Services

Greenfield, Stanley R. *National Directory of Addresses and Telephone Numbers.* New York: Bantam Books, 1977.

The Consumer Information Catalog. Pueblo: U.S. General Services Administration, published annually.

14. Automobiles

Back Yard Mechanic, Vols. 1 & 2. Washington, D.C.: U.S. Superintendant of Public Documents, 1978.

Sclar, Donna. *Auto Repair for Dummies.* New York: McGraw-Hill Book Company, 1976.

Index